KINGS & QUEENS
OF BRITAIN'S GOLDEN AGE

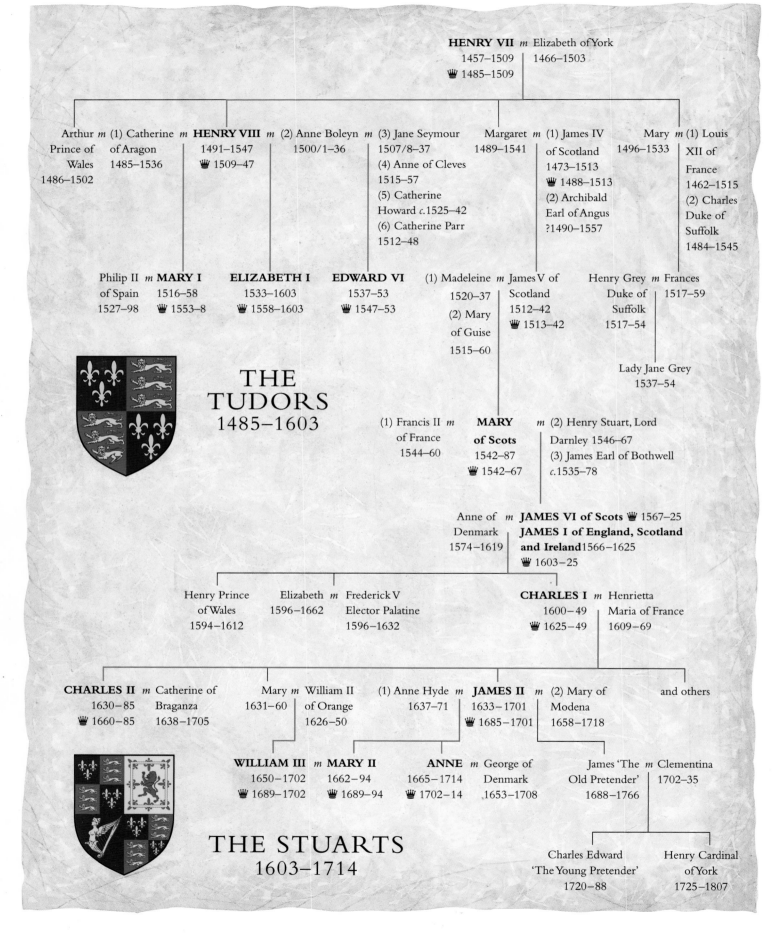

HENRY VII *m* Elizabeth of York
1457–1509   1466–1503
♛ 1485–1509

Arthur *m* (1) Catherine *m* **HENRY VIII** *m* (2) Anne Boleyn *m* (3) Jane Seymour   Margaret *m* (1) James IV   Mary *m* (1) Louis
Prince of   of Aragon   1491–1547   1500/1–36   1507/8–37   1489–1541   of Scotland   1496–1533   XII of
Wales   1485–1536   ♛ 1509–47   (4) Anne of Cleves   1473–1513   France
1486–1502   1515–57   ♛ 1488–1513   1462–1515
(5) Catherine   (2) Archibald   (2) Charles
Howard *c.*1525–42   Earl of Angus   Duke of
(6) Catherine Parr   ?1490–1557   Suffolk
1512–48   1484–1545

Philip II *m* **MARY I**   **ELIZABETH I**   **EDWARD VI**   (1) Madeleine *m* James V of   Henry Grey *m* Frances
of Spain   1516–58   1533–1603   1537–53   1520–37   Scotland   Duke of   1517–59
1527–98   ♛ 1553–8   ♛ 1558–1603   ♛ 1547–53   (2) Mary   1512–42   Suffolk
of Guise   ♛ 1513–42   1517–54
1515–60

Lady Jane Grey
1537–54

THE
TUDORS
1485–1603

(1) Francis II *m*   **MARY**   *m* (2) Henry Stuart, Lord
of France   **of Scots**   Darnley 1546–67
1544–60   1542–87   (3) James Earl of Bothwell
♛ 1542–67   *c.*1535–78

Anne of *m* **JAMES VI of Scots** ♛ 1567–25
Denmark   **JAMES I of England, Scotland**
1574–1619   **and Ireland** 1566–1625
♛ 1603–25

Henry Prince   Elizabeth *m* Frederick V   **CHARLES I** *m* Henrietta
of Wales   1596–1662   Elector Palatine   1600–49   Maria of France
1594–1612   1596–1632   ♛ 1625–49   1609–69

CHARLES II *m* Catherine of   Mary *m* William II   (1) Anne Hyde *m* **JAMES II** *m* (2) Mary of   and others
1630–85   Braganza   1631–60   of Orange   1637–71   1633–1701   Modena
♛ 1660–85   1638–1705   1626–50   ♛ 1685–1701   1658–1718

WILLIAM III *m* **MARY II**   **ANNE** *m* George of   James 'The *m* Clementina
1650–1702   1662–94   1665–1714   Denmark   Old Pretender'   1702–35
♛ 1689–1702   ♛ 1689–94   ♛ 1702–14   1653–1708   1688–1766

THE STUARTS
1603–1714

Charles Edward   Henry Cardinal
'The Young Pretender'   of York
1720–88   1725–1807

KINGS & QUEENS
OF BRITAIN'S GOLDEN AGE

THE TUDORS AND STUARTS: 1485–1714
FROM HENRY VIII TO ELIZABETH I, CHARLES I AND QUEEN ANNE

CHARLES PHILLIPS
CONSULTANT: DR JOHN HAYWOOD

southwater

This edition is published by Southwater, an imprint of Anness Publishing Ltd, Hermes House, 88–89 Blackfriars Road, London SE1 8HA; tel. 020 7401 2077; fax 020 7633 9499

www.southwaterbooks.com; www.annesspublishing.com

Anness Publishing has a new picture agency outlet for images for publishing, promotions or advertising. Please visit our website www.practicalpictures.com for more information.

UK agent: The Manning Partnership Ltd; tel. 01225 478444; fax 01225 478440; sales@manning-partnership.co.uk
UK distributor: Grantham Book Services Ltd; tel. 01476 541080; fax 01476 541061; orders@gbs.tbs-ltd.co.uk
North American agent/distributor: National Book Network; tel 301 459 3366; fax 301 429 5746; www.nbnbooks.com
Australian agent/distributor: Pan Macmillan Australia; tel. 1300 135 113; fax 1300 135 103; customer.service@macmillan.com.au
New Zealand agent/distributor: David Bateman Ltd; tel. (09) 415 7664; fax (09) 415 8892

Publisher: Joanna Lorenz
Senior Managing Editor: Conor Kilgallon
Editor: Joy Wotton
Consultants: Dr John Haywood, Stephen Slater
Designer: Nigel Partridge
Illustrators: Anthony Duke and Rob Highton
Production Controller: Wendy Lawson

ETHICAL TRADING POLICY

Previously published as part of a larger volume, *The Complete Illustrated Guide to the Kings & Queens of Britain*

PICTURE ACKNOWLEDGEMENTS
The Art Archive: 16b, 22t, 35c, 43t, 61b, 68b, 70t&b, 72t, 75t, 79tr /Army and Navy Club/ Eileen Tweedy 81tr /Bodleian Library, Oxford 16t, 53t /British Library 2, 17bl /British Library/ HarperCollins Publishers 17t /Christ's Hospital/Eileen Tweedy 76-7 /Cornelius de Vries 25t /Culver Pictures 61t /Dagli Orti 17br /Doges' Palace, Venice/Dagli Orti 21bl /Galleria degli Uffizi, Florence/Dagli Orti 26b /Galleria Sabauda, Turin/Dagli Orti 67bl /Jarrold Publishing 25b, 29tl, 55b /Musee Calvet, Avignon/Dagli Orti 20t /Musée de la Marine, Paris/Dagli Orti 48t /Musée des Beaux Arts, Lausanne/Dagli Orti 44 /Musée du Château de Versailles/ Dagli Orti 6-7, 42bl, 52t /Museo del Prado, Madrid/Dagli Orti 9t, 35b /Palazzo Barberini, Rome/ Dagli Orti 22b /Palazzo Pitti, Florence/Dagli Orti 40, 64b, 74b /Plymouth Art Gallery/Eileen Tweedy 47b /Society of Apothecaries/Eileen Tweedy 47t /Tate Gallery, London 91 /University Library, Geneva/Dagli Orti 59b /Victoria & Albert Museum/Sally Chappell 46t, 51b /Windsor Castle 1, 31
The Bridgeman Art Library: /Ashmolean Museum, University of Oxford 65t /Bibliotheque Municipale, Arras, France 20b /Bolton Museum and Art Gallery, Lancs 86 /British Library, London 79b /British Library, London/Giraudon 63t /British Museum, London 89t /Burghley House Collection, Lincs 54t&b /Chateau de Versailles, France/Flammarion, Giraudon 92b /Collection of the Earl of Pembroke, Wilton House, Wilts 30b, 32t /Corsham Court, Wilts 55t /Czartoryski Museum, Cracow, Poland 45tl /Falkland Palace, Falkland, Fife 8bl /Fitzwilliam Museum, University of Cambridge 74t /Geffrye Museum, London 81tl /Harrogate Museums and Art Gallery 59tr /Heini Schneebeli: 92t /Hever Castle Ltd, Kent 8br /Ipswich Borough Council Museums & Galleries 24t /Kunsthistorisches Museum, Vienna 26tr; 48b, 49t /Lambeth Palace Library, London 42tr /Louvre, Paris/Giraudon 27tl /Massachusetts Historical Society, Boston, MA 68t /Timothy Millet Collection 67b /Philip Mould, Historical Portraits Ltd, London 72bl /Museum of Fine Arts, Houston, Texas, USA 62t /Museum of London 78, 89b /Museum of the City of New York 83t /National Gallery, London 35, 69b /National Museum and Gallery of Wales 18-19 /National Portrait Gallery, London 27b, 28, 33b, 34, 39t /John Noott Galleries, Broadway, Worcs 83b /Private Collection 32tr, 36-7, 50b, 53b, 59tc, 60t, 63b, 66, 72br, 73, 75b, 82t, 84t, 87b, 90, 93t, 94b, 95b /Private Collection, Ackermann and Johnson Ltd, London 85t /Private Collection, Boltin Picture Library 8t /Private Collection, Bonhams 95t /Private Collection, Christie's Images 85b /Private Collection, Mark Fiennes 30t /Private Collection, Philip Mould, Historical Portraits Ltd, London 26tl, 82b /Private Collection, The Stapleton Collection 21t, 27tr, 29tr, 45tr, 49b, 50t, 67tl /Private Collection, Ken Welsh 38, 41tl, 51t, 52b /Royal Hospital Chelsea, London 69t, 80 /Royal Naval College, Greenwich, London 88t /Scottish National Portrait Gallery, Edinburgh 94 /St Paul's Cathedral Library, London 84b /Society of Antiquaries, London 65b /South African National Gallery, Cape Town 87t /St Faith's Church, Gaywood, Norfolk 46b /Stapleton Collection 81b /The Crown Estate 58 /The Drambuie Collection, Edinburgh 93b /The Trustees of the Weston Park Foundation 33t, 56-7 /Traquair House, Innerleithen 43b /Victoria & Albert Museum, London 41tr /Walker Art Gallery, National Museums Liverpool 39b /Westminster Abbey, London 21br /Yale Center for British Art, Paul Mellon Collection 9b, 41b, 62b, 79tl
Mary Evans Picture Library 23, 24b, 38b, 88b
Rex Features: 3

p. 1 Henry VIII. p. 2 Family Tree of the Houses of Tudor and Stuart., tracing the Royal Line of Succession. p. 3 The Imperial State Crown. pp. 4–5 (top): shields of William I, Stephen, Henry II, Edward III, the House of Stewart, James I, William III and Anne. (bottom): coins of Henry VII, Henry VIII, Edward VI, Elizabeth I, James I, Charles I, Charles II and Anne.

CONTENTS

INTRODUCTION

The House of Tudor gave England its two most charismatic monarchs: Henry VIII, the king who married six wives and established the Church of England, and his daughter Elizabeth I, whose reign saw the first flowering of William Shakespeare's genius and the defeat of the Spanish Armada. These years of greatness were followed by the establishment of the House of Stuart in Britain and decades of turmoil. Within fifty years of Elizabeth's death in 1603, the monarchy was brought to brief extinction with the execution of Charles I by Parliament in 1649 and the overthrow of his son James II. However, the Restoration of Charles II and the reign of William III and Mary II led to a new golden age for Britain's monarchy.

Left: Henry VIII attended the Anglo-French summit at the Field of the Cloth of Gold, near Calais, in 1520. A city of sumptuous pavilions was erected and the fountains flowed constantly with red wine.

TUDORS AND STUARTS

On 30 November 1601 Queen Elizabeth I made a celebrated speech to a representative group of MPs. Elizabeth was at the time 68 years old, and she had been on the throne for 43 years. As she drew towards the end of a reign of magnificent achievements for her country, a reign that would give its name to the 'Elizabethan age', she was popularly and officially revered as the 'Virgin Queen', 'married' to her country and tied to her people by bonds of love and gratitude.

GOD'S INSTRUMENT

Elizabeth's words that day celebrated these bonds of love and gratitude and came to be known as her 'golden speech'. She declared: 'There is no jewel, be it of never so rich a price, which I set before this jewel: I mean your love. For I do esteem it more than any treasure or riches; for that we know how to prize, but love and thanks I count invaluable … I have cause to wish nothing more than to content the subject and that is a duty which I owe. Neither do I desire to live longer

Below: Mary Queen of Scots was queen at the age of seven days in 1542, but was forced to abdicate, aged 24, in 1567.

days than I may see your prosperity and that is my only desire. And as I am that person still yet, under God, hath delivered you and so I trust by the almighty power of God that I shall be his instrument to preserve you from every peril, dishonour, shame, tyranny and oppression, partly by means of your intended helps which we take very acceptably because it manifesteth the largeness of your good loves and loyalties unto your sovereign'.

ENGLAND'S GLORIANA

The relationship of queen and subjects celebrated in these memorable words may be likened to that of a mother and her loyal offspring – a connection sustained by deep feelings of love and duty. The queen loved and was loved: her behaviour was bound by her sense of duty to her subjects and also to God, whose chosen instrument of government she was.

The queen's speech was, of course, propaganda: it represented an idealised image of Elizabeth's interaction with her subjects and government through Parliament. Yet it captured the romance of the Elizabethan age, of years in which such illustrious men as Sir Francis Drake carried the name of England and her queen to far-flung corners of the world, and the poet Edmund Spenser was led to immortalise 'the most excellent and person of our sovereign the Queen' in Gloriana, the heroine of his epic poem "The Faerie Queene". Elizabeth, last and greatest of the Tudor monarchs, was feted by her people.

THE MONARCHY ABOLISHED

If the relationship of the monarch with MPs and people could be represented as a chaste love affair towards the close of Elizabeth's reign, it was a love affair that soured quickly under the

Above: Henry VIII (1509–47) ruled through council and other instruments of government, but his will was not to be crossed.

strain of attempts by Elizabeth's Stuart successors – the Scottish king James I and his son Charles I – to rule with absolute authority. On 22 November 1641 – just 40 years after Elizabeth

Below: Mother to her people. Elizabeth I (1558–1603), who never married, was promoted as a Protestant 'Madonna'.

pronounced the honeyed words of her 'golden speech' – the House of Commons passed by 159 to 148 votes a 'Grand Remonstrance' or complaint against Charles I, listing the many failings of his government and for the first time in English history making it clear that Parliament would take steps to remove a king who was guilty of abuses of power.

The scene was set for the Civil War. Within a decade, Charles was tried for committing treason against his own people, sentenced to death and executed – and Parliament voted, on 17 March 1649, to abolish the monarchy and make England a 'Commonwealth and free state'.

But England's experiment with republicanism was brief. On 8 May 1660 Parliament declared Charles Stuart, the son of the executed King Charles I, King of England: he was greeted by cheering crowds and pealing church bells when he entered London on 29 May that year.

THE POWER OF PARLIAMENT
Acclaimed though he was on his triumphant return, Charles II became king at the invitation of Parliament, and a result of a carefully plotted political

Below: Return of the House of Stuart. Eleven years after Charles I's execution, Charles II regained the crown in 1660.

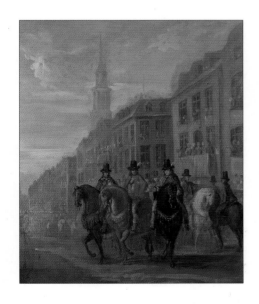

settlement, after MPs accepted Charles's pledges in a declaration that was made in Breda in the Low Countries on 4 April 1660 – among other things to issue a general pardon and the guarantee liberty of conscience in religion.

This settlement collapsed with astonishing speed in the reign of Charles's brother, James II, whose actions convinced many people that he was set on restoring the Roman Catholic faith in England. He fled into exile in France and was formally deposed by Parliament on 23 December 1688.

JOINT MONARCHS
In 1688, Parliament acted to secure a Protestant future for the country, calling on James's eldest daughter

Above: Divine right. In 1598 James VI of Scots (later James I of England) declared that kings were instruments of God's will.

Princess Mary and her husband Prince William of Orange, both Protestants, to occupy the throne.

At their joint coronation on 11 April 1689 as William III and Mary II, they swore the new oaths of a 'constitutional monarchy' wherein the real power lay with the elected MPs rather than leading members of a hereditary royal family. They swore to rule in line with 'the statutes of Parliament' and – as all their successors, down to Elizabeth II in 1953 have done – to 'maintain in the United Kingdom the Protestant Reformed Religion established by law'.

POMP AND PAGEANTRY

Public royal ceremony celebrates the ruling king or queen as the kingdom's most majestic individual, elevated far above even the proudest and noblest of subjects. Across centuries, the monarchy has emphasized its pre-eminence through a wide range of magnificent ceremonies – including ordination-coronation rites, royal weddings and funerals, reviews of the armed forces, triumphal processions or 'progresses' and elaborate social activities at court.

CORONATION CEREMONIAL

The coronation of King Edgar in Bath on 11 May 973 was the first at which an English monarch was anointed with oil. The ceremony emphasized Edgar's sacred calling and was deliberately reminiscent of a priest's ordination. It was marked by a public celebration of Edgar's earthly supremacy. The coronation of Henry VII, the founder of the Tudor dynasty, followed the tradition established by Edgar in 973. On 30 October 1485 Henry VII, who had won the crown in battle from King Richard III at Bosworth Field, attempted to add legitimacy to his rule by holding a coronation ceremony of the utmost splendour.

King Henry VIII was crowned in a magnificent joint coronation at Westminster Abbey with his wife Catherine of Aragon, on 24 June 1509. This was followed by a banquet in Westminster Hall and a week of ceremonial jousting. Henry's son, Edward VI, was crowned at Westminster on 20 February 1547. Elizabeth's coronation at Westminster Abbey was marked by her refusal to witness the Catholic ritual of Bishop Oglethorpe elevating the Host.

Above: The gold used in St Edward's Crown may have come from Edward the Confessor's crown. The Sceptre with the Cross contains the world's largest top-quality cut diamond, the Cullinan I. The Sceptre with the Dove, the Orb and the Ring are also shown.

Conflict also marked Charles I's coronation in 1626, which his French wife, Henrietta Maria, refused to attend because the ceremony was performed by a Protestant bishop. His son Charles II's coronation was a fine spectacle with theatrical tableaux and a splendid feast. The Hanoverian kings maintained magnificent coronation ceremonies. George IV spent some £240,000 celebrating his coronation in 1820. Such extravagance led to a backlash – William IV had a low-key coronation in 1831 – but from the late Victorian period onwards pomp and glory returned. In 1911 King George V was lavishly crowned twice – once in Westminster Abbey in London and once in India, as its Emperor.

Left: Edinburgh Castle dominates the skyline, just as it has dominated Scottish history as a stronghold and seat of kings.

Right: The west front of Westminster Abbey, which has seen the coronations and funerals of many English and British monarchs.

BRITAIN'S CROWN JEWELS

The Crown Jewels are kept in the Jewel House at the Tower of London. The jewels have had a troubled history. The first monarch to collect royal regalia was probably Edward the Confessor, but this first collection was lost by King John in quicksand as he tried to cross the Wash, a tidal estuary in eastern England, in 1216. A replacement set was made, but following the execution of Charles I Oliver Cromwell ordered its destruction. Then another new set was made at a cost of £12,185 for the Restoration of the Monarchy in 1660, although some earlier pieces – such as the 12th-century Coronation Spoon – were recovered and returned to Charles II.

At the climax of the coronation service, after taking the coronation oath and being anointed with holy oil using the Coronation Spoon, the monarch is handed the Sovereign's Orb, fitted with the Coronation Ring, given the Sceptre with the Cross and the Sceptre with the Dove and then crowned with St Edward's Crown. Most of these treasures date to the Restoration; but the gold in St Edward's Crown may have come from Edward the Confessor's crown and the Coronation Ring is from William IV's crowning in 1831. The Imperial State Crown was made in 1937 for George VI's coronation.

FUNERAL RITES

Another lavish event as a reign begins is the celebration of the previous monarch's life with a funeral procession and burial in an elaborate tomb. In times of disputed successions, an imposing funeral could make a public statement, suggesting a new ruler was a suitable successor. Thus, on the day of his own coronation (6 January 1066), Harold II held a funeral procession for Edward the Confessor, who was buried before the High Altar in Westminster Abbey.

In the early years of the Tudor dynasty Henry VIII laid on a grand state funeral for his father Henry VII, with a procession of 600 candle-bearers, the royal choir, and a host of churchmen, all led by Sir Edward Howard mounted on a horse and carrying the royal banner. King Henry VII was laid in a vault in the Lady Chapel he had created in the Abbey; Henry VIII oversaw the creation of a magnificent gilt bronze tomb effigy of his father and mother, created by Florentine sculptor Pietro Torrigiano – and one of the finest Renaissance works on art in England.

On the death of Elizabeth I, James VI and I erected tombs at Westminster Abbey for her and his mother, Mary, Queen of Scots. In 1901, Edward VII paid tribute to his mother Queen Victoria with the grandest of state funerals. Almost 101 years later in 2002, Queen Elizabeth the Queen Mother was remembered by her daughter Elizabeth II in a grand state funeral at Westminster Abbey.

ROYAL WEDDINGS

Because they have often brought about the union of two ruling houses, royal weddings have required magnificent ceremony – not only to impress the people, but also to honour the king or queen's new royal in-laws. When James IV of Scotland married Princess Margaret of England, daughter of Henry VII, on 8 August 1503, celebrations at Holyrood Palace in Edinburgh included pageants, jousting tournaments and wine-fuelled banquets – and the marriage was marked by the publication of the poem "The Thistle and the Rose", by leading Scots poet William Dunbar.

In the modern era, coronations, weddings, funerals and other aspects of royal pageantry – such as Elizabeth II's Silver and Golden Jubilee celebrations, the Trooping of the Colour and State Opening of Parliament – have assumed importance as symbolic enactments of the greatness of the country's and the monarchy's history.

TIMELINE OF MONARCHS

1485–1532

22 Aug 1485 Henry Tudor's victory at Bosworth Field makes him Henry VII. He inaugurates the royal house of Tudor.

14 Nov 1501 Henry VII's eldest son and heir, Prince Arthur, marries Catherine of Aragon.

2 Apr 1502 Arthur, Prince of Wales, dies, making his younger brother Henry heir to the throne.

8 Aug 1503 Henry VII's daughter, Margaret Tudor, marries King William IV of Scots.

21 Apr 1509 Henry VII dies and is succeeded by Henry VIII.

11 June 1509 Henry VIII marries his late brother Arthur's widow, Catherine of Aragon.

9 Sept 1513 King James IV of Scots is killed during an attempted invasion of England at Flodden, Northumberland.

18 Feb 1516 Catherine of Aragon gives birth to a daughter, the future Queen Mary.

June 1520 King Henry VIII holds a peace summit with King Francis I of France at the 'Field of the Cloth of Gold' near Calais.

c.1527 Henry, desperate to father a legitimate male heir, decides that his marriage to Catherine of Aragon was not legitimate because she had first wed his brother Arthur.

13 July 1529 Pope Clement VII orders that King Henry VIII's case for divorce from Catherine of Aragon must be heard in Rome.

1533–1540

24 Jan 1533 Henry secretly marries his mistress Anne Boleyn.

23 May 1533 Archbishop of Canterbury Thomas Cranmer declares Henry's marriage to Catherine of Aragon invalid.

1 June 1533 Henry VIII's second wife, Anne Boleyn, is crowned Queen.

7 Sept 1533 Anne Boleyn gives birth to a daughter, the future Elizabeth I.

30 Apr 1534 The Act of Succession annuls Henry VIII's marriage to Catherine of Aragon and makes Anne Boleyn's daughter Elizabeth heir to the throne.

28 Nov 1534 The Act of Supremacy makes Henry 'the only supreme head of the Church of England'.

2 May 1536 Accusing his second wife Anne Boleyn of adultery, Henry imprisons her in the Tower of London.

19 May 1536 Convicted of adultery, Anne Boleyn is beheaded.

30 May 1536 Henry marries his third wife, Jane Seymour.

1536-37 A Roman Catholic revolt in northern England, the 'Pilgrimage of Grace for the Commonweal', is put down.

12 Oct 1537 Jane Seymour gives birth to a baby boy, the future King Edward VI.

24 Oct 1537 Jane Seymour dies.

1539 King Henry VIII sponsors the publication of the 'Great Bible' in English.

6 Jan 1540 Henry VIII weds his fourth wife, Princess Anne of Cleves, in a diplomatic marriage.

Mar 1540 Waltham Abbey is the last English religious house to be closed down in King Henry's 'Dissolution of the Monasteries' (1536-40).

28 July 1540 After divorcing Anne of Cleves, Henry marries his fifth wife, Catherine Howard.

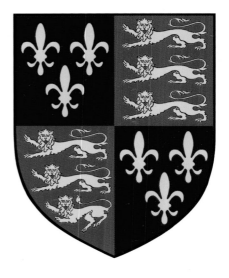

Above: Henry VIII.

1541–1553

13 Feb 1542 Denounced as 'unchaste', Catherine Howard is beheaded.

14 Dec 1542 James V of Scots is succeeded by his baby daughter Mary.

12 July 1543 Henry VIII of England marries his sixth wife, Catherine Parr.

28 Jan 1547 Henry dies and is succeeded by his only son, Edward VI.

1549 The First Book of Common Prayer is published.

1552 The Second Book of Common Prayer is published.

6 July 1553 Edward VI dies.

10 July 1553 Lady Jane Grey is proclaimed Queen.

19 July 1553 Edward VI's sister Mary deposes Jane and is proclaimed queen.

1 Oct 1553 Mary is crowned as England's first reigning queen.

Above: Henry VII.

Above: Henry VIII.

1554–1599

25 July 1554 Mary I weds Philip of Spain, son of Charles V, Holy Roman Emperor and king of Spain.

30 Nov 1554 Papal legate Cardinal Reginald Pole pronounces absolution on England, formally reconciling the country to the papacy.

21 Mar 1556 Thomas Cranmer, former Archbishop of Canterbury, is burnt at the stake.

24 Apr 1558 Mary, Queen of Scots marries the Dauphin Francis, heir to the French throne.

17 Nov 1558 Mary I dies, leaving the throne to her Protestant sister Elizabeth.

1559 The Acts of Supremacy and Uniformity reintroduce Protestantism in England.

5 Dec 1560 Francis II, King of France and husband of Mary Queen of Scots, dies at the age of 16.

19 Aug 1561 Mary Queen of Scots returns from France to Scotland.

24 July 1567 Mary Queen of Scots abdicates in the face of rebellion.

29 July 1567 James Stuart, the infant son of Mary Queen of Scots, is crowned King James VI of Scots at Stirling.

1569 A Roman Catholic uprising in the north of England is mercilessly put down by Elizabeth.

Feb 1570 Pope Pius V excommunicates Queen Elizabeth.

4 Apr 1581 Elizabeth knights Francis Drake in honour of his circumnavigation of the world.

8 Feb 1587 Mary, Queen of Scots, who has been in captivity since she fled to England in 1568, is beheaded at Fotheringhay Castle, Northamptonshire. She had been found guilty of complicity in a plot to assassinate Elizabeth.

1588 The Spanish Armada is defeated. Elizabeth addresses soldiers at Tilbury: 'I myself will be your general, judge and rewarder of every one of your virtues in the field'.

Above: Stewart.

1600–1605

1601 In her so-called 'Golden Speech' to Parliament, Elizabeth declares: 'I do not so much rejoice that God hath made me to be a Queen, as to be a Queen over so thankful a people … It is my desire to live nor reign no longer than my life and reign shall be for your good.'

24 Mar 1603 Elizabeth dies at Richmond Palace and is succeeded by King James VI of Scots.

25 July 1603 James is crowned King James I in Westminster Abbey. His reign inaugurates the English rule of the House of Stuart.

20 Oct 1604 James declares himself 'King of Great Britain'.

5 Nov 1605 The pro-Catholic 'Gunpowder Plot' led by Francis Tresham and Guy Fawkes is foiled.

Above: Edward VI.

Above: James I.

1606–1620

12 Apr 1606 A new Anglo-Scottish flag is called the 'Union Jack' from the French form, 'Jacques', of King James I's name.

13 May 1607 English settlers found 'Jamestown' in Virginia.

1611 The 'King James Version' of the Bible published.

1616 The daughter of a Native American chief, Pocahontas, meets King James at court.

16 Sept 1620 The Mayflower, bearing 101 Puritans seeking freedom from religious persecution at the hands of King James and the Church of England, departs from Plymouth, bound for North America.

26 Dec 1620 Mayflower pilgrims found settlement of New Plymouth.

Above: Elizabeth.

Above: Anne.

1621–1649

1624 Virginia, in North America, becomes the King's Royal Colony.
27 Mar 1625 James I dies and is succeeded by his son, Charles I.
2 Feb 1626 Charles is crowned in Westminster Abbey.
23 Aug 1628 Royal favourite the duke of Buckingham is assassinated.
1638-49 Political and religious tensions, exacerbated by Charles's attempts at absolute rule, result in Civil War.
20-27 Jan 1649 Charles is tried as a tyrant and traitor.
30 Jan 1649 King Charles is executed.
8 Feb 1649 Charles is buried in St George's Chapel, Windsor.
17 Mar 1649 MPs pass an act abolishing the monarchy and making England a 'Commonwealth and free state'.

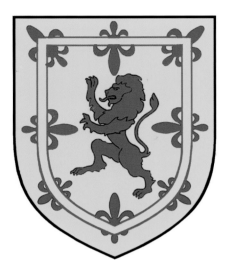

Above: The House of Stewart.

1650–1661

1 Jan 1651 In defiance of the abolition of the monarchy, Charles I's son, Charles Stuart, is crowned King Charles II of England, Scotland, Ireland and France at Scone, Scotland.
14 Oct 1651 Charles flees to France after his invasion of England ends in defeat at the Battle of Worcester.
16 Dec 1653 Oliver Cromwell is made 'Lord Protector'.
3 Sept 1658 Oliver Cromwell dies. He is succeeded as Protector by his son, Richard.
2 May 1660 Charles Stuart is recalled by Parliament.
29 May 1660 Charles enters London in triumph as the monarchy is restored.
23 April 1661 Charles is crowned King Charles II in Westminster Abbey.

1662–1687

22 May 1662 Charles II marries a Roman Catholic, Princess Catherine of Braganza, the daughter of the King of Portugal.
24 Mar 1663 Charles grants North American lands of 'Carolina' to eight wealthy noblemen.
8 Jul 1663 Charles grants a royal charter to Rhode Island colony.
2–6 Sept 1666 During the Great Fire of London, Charles fights the flames on the streets alongside his subjects.
1678 Former priest Titus Oates alleges a Roman Catholic plot to kill the king.
1681 Charles II grants lands of Pennsylvania to Quaker William Penn.
1683 The 'Rye House Plot' to kill Charles is foiled.
6 Feb 1685 King Charles I dies, after reputedly converting to Roman Catholicism on his deathbed. He is succeeded by his brother, the Roman Catholic James, duke of York, who becomes James II.
23 Apr 1685 King James II is crowned in Westminster Abbey.
6 July 1685 A royalist army defeats the Protestant duke of Monmouth at the Battle of Sedgemoor.
4 April 1687 James issues the Declaration of Indulgence, which suspends laws against Roman Catholics and other dissenters from the Church of England.
3 July 1687 James formally receives the papal nuncio Cardinal Adda.

Above: James I.

Above: James I.

Above: Oliver Cromwell, Lord Protector.

1688–1690

10 June 1688 James's son, Prince James Francis Edward, is born.

30 June 1688 Nobles call on Prince William of Orange, the Protestant husband of James's eldest daughter Mary, to invade to secure the Protestant succession to the throne.

5 Nov 1688 William of Orange lands at Torbay.

23 Dec 1688 James II flees England and is formally deposed as king by Parliament.

28 Jan 1689 Parliament declares the throne vacant following the flight of James.

13 Feb 1689 William of Orange and Mary are offered the crown under a Bill of Rights that makes the monarchy subject to Parliament.

11 Apr 1689 William III and his wife Mary II are crowned as king and queen in Westminster Abbey. They swear the new coronation vows of the 'constitutional monarchy'.

27 July 1689 'Jacobite' supporters of James II clash with royalist supporters of William and Mary at Killiecrankie in Scotland.

21 Aug 1689 Royalists are victorious at the Battle of Dunkeld.

1689–1690 During the bloody siege of Londonderry, Ireland, by James's II's army, Protestants within the city introduce the enduring slogan 'No surrender'.

1 July 1690 William defeats James at the Battle of the Boyne, Ireland.

Above: William III.

1691–1714

3 Oct 1691 The Irish 'Williamite war', decided in William's favour by the Battle of the Boyne, is ended by the Treaty of Limerick.

28 Dec 1694 Queen Mary dies at Kensington Palace and is buried in Westminster Abbey.

31 Dec 1694 A griefstricken King William breaks down before Parliament.

Feb 1695 William acknowledges James II's second daughter, Anne, as his heir.

30 July 1700 Anne's only son, William Duke of Gloucester dies aged 11.

12 June 1701 Parliament passes the Act of Settlement, which nominates a Protestant heir to follow Anne: Sophia, Electress of Hanover, daughter of Charles I's sister Elizabeth and her husband Frederick V the Elector Palatinate.

Above: Anne.

6 Sept 1701 The exiled King James II dies at St Germain, France.

8 Mar 1702 King William dies. He is buried in Westminster Abbey.

23 April 1702 Queen Anne is crowned in Westminster Abbey.

16 Jan 1707 The Scottish Parliament approves the Act of Union, which creates the United Kingdom of Great Britain.

6 Mar 1707 Queen Anne gives royal assent to the Act of Union.

Mar 1708 James Francis Edward Stuart, son of the late deposed king James II, bungles an attempted invasion as his fleet fails to land in Scotland.

1 Aug 1714 Queen Anne dies at Kensington Palace and is buried at Westminster Abbey on 24 Aug.

Above: Charles I.

Above: Charles II.

Above: Anne.

BRITISH MONARCHS

This list of monarchs names the kings and queens of Britain from the time of the ancient rulers of England and Scotland to the present day.

Much of the monarchy's authority and prestige derives from its ancient roots, from the centuries of historical continuity celebrated in genealogical and dynastic tables. Yet there are countless examples of force of arms and political manoeuvring intervening in dynastic or designated succession. In 1066, Duke William of Normandy famously had to enforce his claim that he was the designated successor of King Edward the Confessor in the face of several rival claims, including that of Harold Godwine, Earl of Wessex, who had himself declared King Harold II and was crowned on the very day after Edward the Confessor's death. William's claim triumphed at the Battle of Hastings.

The great Scottish national hero Robert the Bruce killed his chief rival to the succession, John Comyn, before having himself crowned King Robert I of Scots. Richard III of England occupied the throne at the expense of his uncrowned nephew, the 12-year-old King Edward V, whom Richard almost certainly had murdered in the Tower of London. Henry VII won the English crown in battle against Richard III ad established the Tudor dynasty.

Throughout these and many other upheavals, the theory of dynastic succession with God's blessing was maintained and all these kings – usurpers or murderers as they might be – laid claim to a dynastic link and were anointed as God's chosen servants on the throne. Henry IV, a usurper, brought an innovation to the coronation in an attempt to legitimize his rule. His ordination was the first to use holy oil reputedly given to Saint Thomas à Becket by the Virgin Mary.

KINGS AND QUEENS OF SCOTLAND (TO 1603)

THE HOUSE OF MACALPINE
Kenneth I mac Alpin 841–859
Donald I 859–863
Constantine I 863–877
Aed Whitefoot 877–878
Eochaid 878–889 (joint)
Giric 878–889
Donald II Dasachtach 889–900
Constantine II 900–943
Malcolm I 943–954
Indulf 954–962
Dubh 962–967
Culen 967–971
Kenneth II 971–995
Constantine III 995–997
Kenneth III 997–1005
Malcolm II 1005–1034

Above: James IV of Scotland presenting arms to his wife Queen Margaret, daughter of King Henry VII of England.

THE HOUSE OF DUNKELD
Duncan I 1034–1040
Macbeth 1040–1057
Lulach 1057–1058
Malcolm III Canmore 1058–1093
Donald III 1093–1094
Duncan II 1094
Donald III 1094–1097 (joint)

Below: King David II of Scotland (left) makes peace with King Edward III of England, in 1357.

Edmund 1094–1097 (joint)
Edgar 1097–1107
Alexander I 1107–1124
David I 1124–1153
Malcolm IV the Maiden 1153–1165
William I the Lion 1165–1214
Alexander II 1214–1249
Alexander III 1249–1286
Margaret, Maid of Norway 1286–1290

THE HOUSE OF BALLIOL
John Balliol 1292–1296

THE HOUSE OF BRUCE
Robert I the Bruce 1306–1329
David II 1329–1332, 1338–1371

THE HOUSE OF BALLIOL
Edward Balliol 1332–1336

THE HOUSE OF STEWART
Robert II 1371–1390
Robert III 1390–1406
James I 1406–1437
James II 1437–1460
James III 1460–1488
James IV 1488–1513
James V 1513–1542
Mary, Queen of Scots 1542–1567
James VI 1567–1603

KINGS AND QUEENS OF ENGLAND

THE HOUSE OF WESSEX

Egbert (802–839)
Aethelwulf (839–858)
Aethelbald (858–860)
Aethelbert (860–865/6)
Aethelred I (865/6–871)
Alfred the Great (871–899)
Edward the Elder (899–924/5)
Athelstan (924/5–939)
Edmund I (939–946)
Eadred (946–955)
Eadwig (955–959)
Edgar (959–975)
Edward the Martyr (975–978)
Aethelred II the Unready (978–1013, 1014–1016)
Edmund Ironside (1016)

THE DANISH LINE

Cnut (1016–1035)
Harald I Hardrada (1035–1040)
Harthacnut (1040–1042)

THE HOUSE OF WESSEX, RESTORED

Edward the Confessor (1042–1066)
Harold II (1066)

THE NORMANS

William I the Conqueror (1066–1087)
William II Rufus (1087–1100)
Henry I (1100–1135)
Stephen (1135–1154)

Above: King John goes riding. Hunting was the sport of kings from William I.

THE PLANTAGENETS

Henry II (1154–1189)
Richard I the Lionheart (1189–1199)
John (1199–1216)
Henry III (1216–1272)
Edward I (1272–1307)
Edward II (1307–1327)
Edward III (1327–1377)
Richard II (1377–1399)

THE HOUSE OF LANCASTER

Henry IV (1399–1413)
Henry V (1413–1422)
Henry VI (1422–1461, 1470–1471)

THE HOUSE OF YORK

Edward IV (1461–1470, 1471–1483)
Edward V (1483)
Richard III (1483–1485)

THE HOUSE OF TUDOR

Henry VII (1485–1509)
Henry VIII (1509–1547)
Edward VI (1547–1553)
Lady Jane Grey (1553)
Mary I (1553–1558)
Elizabeth I (1558–1603)

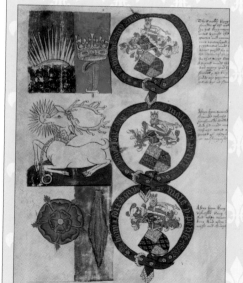

Left: The heraldic badges of Kings Edward III, Richard II and Henry IV from Writhe's Garter Book.

KINGS AND QUEENS OF GREAT BRITAIN

THE HOUSE OF STUART

James I (1603–1625)
Charles I (1625–1649)
Charles II (1660–1685)
James II (1685–1688)
William III and Mary II (1689–1694)
William III (1689–1702)
Anne (1702–1714)

THE HOUSE OF HANOVER

George I (1714–1727)
George II (1727–1760)
George III (1760–1820)
George IV (1820–1830)
William IV (1830–1837)
Victoria (1837–1901)

THE HOUSE OF SAXE-COBURG-GOTHA

Edward VII (1901–1910)

THE HOUSE OF WINDSOR

George V (1910–1936)
Edward VIII (1936)
George VI (1936–1952)
Elizabeth II (1952–)

Below: The Archbishop of Canterbury reverently places the crown on George V's head at the coronation in 1911.

CHAPTER ONE

THE HOUSE OF TUDOR

1485–1558

In defeating Richard III and claiming the crown at Bosworth Field, Henry VII not only founded the Tudor dynasty but also won final victory for the Lancastrians in their decades-long struggle against the House of York for the English crown.

The House of Tudor encompassed the reigns of five monarchs – Henry VII, Henry VIII, Edward VI, Mary I and Elizabeth I – across 118 years, 1485–1603. The Tudors reigned during a time of religious turmoil, when the European Reformation created the new cultural and intellectual force of Protestantism. In England, Catholics and Protestants struggled for control of the country's future and hundreds of men and women were executed for holding true to new or traditional religious beliefs. These were years, too, of magnificent cultural achievement and enduring fame: when Christopher Marlowe and William Shakespeare were at work and England was beginning to look abroad to the 'New World' of North America.

In these years, the monarchy exercized a more concentrated, centralized authority than ever before, and came to be far less dependent on the support of leading nobles. Arising from the ashes of the Wars of the Roses, the Tudors claimed to give the country a secure and lasting foundation for prosperity: providing an heir and a stable succession became a Tudor obsession. Ultimately, however, the House of Tudor was undone by the lack of an heir. The crown passed out of the Tudor line on the death of Queen Elizabeth, to the first Stuart monarch: King James VI of Scots and I of England.

Left: The Tudor Succession. Henry VIII seated, with Edward VI kneeling on his left, Mary I (left, with her husband, Philip of Spain) and (right) his daughter Elizabeth I.

HENRY VII
1485–1509

Henry Tudor's defeat of Richard III at Bosworth Field was decisive. The battle ushered in the new Tudor dynasty and brought to an end 30 years of dynastic feuding in the Wars of the Roses. Over the ensuing 12 months, Henry proved himself an astute and resourceful king in consolidating a somewhat tenuous grip on the crown. For although he had invaded Richard III's kingdom as representative of the Lancastrian cause, his claim to the throne was relatively weak (he was descended through the female line from Edward III's fourth son John of Gaunt, first Duke of Lancaster).

CONSOLIDATING POWER

The new king's position had been strengthened by the death of the principal Yorkist figureheads, the 'princes in the Tower' Edward V and Richard, Duke of York. To be on the safe side, however, the day after Bosworth, Henry seized and imprisoned in the Tower the next in the Yorkist line to the throne,

Below: The imposter Perkin Warbeck who was adopted by Henry VII's Yorkist foes. He was coached in aristocratic manners by Margaret, sister of Edward IV.

Edward, Earl of Warwick, 15-year-old son of Edward IV's brother George, Duke of Clarence. It was also an advantage that many of Richard III's most important supporters had been killed with him at Bosworth Field.

Henry now determined to bolster his position by attempting to bring an end to Yorkist and Lancastrian rivalries, initially through marriage. During his exile in Brittany, he had pledged to marry Elizabeth, daughter of Edward IV and heiress of the Yorkist cause. Following his coronation as Henry VII in October 1485, he married Elizabeth in Westminster Abbey in January 1486. In March, Henry received papal dispensation for the match, which was against strict church law because the couple were first cousins. The document sent by Pope Innocent stated further that any who rebelled against Henry and his heirs would be excommunicated. As a symbol of the newfound spirit of reconciliation, Henry's personal device, the Tudor Rose, combined the white rose of York and the red rose of Lancaster.

YORKIST PRETENDERS

Henry still faced two Yorkist challenges in the first decade of his reign. The first arose in 1487, when an Oxford joiner's

Above: A watchful eye. Philosopher Sir Francis Bacon wrote of Henry, 'He was a prince sad, serious and full of thoughts.'

son named Lambert Simnel was promoted by Yorkists as Edward, Earl of Warwick, despite the fact that the real Earl of Warwick was in the Tower of London. Simnel was crowned Edward VI in Dublin, in May 1487, then landed with a Yorkist army in Lancashire on 4 June. Henry and his army marched to

HENRY VII, KING OF ENGLAND, 1485–1509

Birth: 28 Jan 1457, Pembroke Castle
Father: Edmund Tudor, 1st Earl of Richmond
Mother: Margaret Beaufort
Accession: 22 Aug 1485
Coronation: 30 Oct 1485, Westminster Abbey
Queen: Elizabeth of York (m. 18 Jan 1486; d. 1503)
Succeeded by: His son Henry VIII
Greatest achievement: Establishing the House of Tudor

16 June 1487: Defeats and captures Pretender Lambert Simnel
Oct 1497: Captures Pretender Perkin Warbeck
1497: Cornishmen revolt over taxes and march on London
14 Nov 1501: Prince Arthur marries Catherine of Aragon
8 Aug 1503: King James IV of Scots weds Henry's daughter Margaret Tudor
Death: 21 April 1509, Richmond Palace, Surrey

QUEST FOR A 'NEW WORLD'

In 1492, Genoese adventurer Christopher Colombus made landfall in the 'New World' of the Caribbean islands with the backing of King Ferdinand of Aragon and Queen Isabella of Castile. Just a few years later, in 1497, another Italian sailor, John Cabot, captained an English voyage of exploration backed by King Henry VII. Cabot, known as Giovanni Caboto in his native land, sailed from Bristol in the *Matthew* in May 1497, made landfall on 24 June on the far side of the Atlantic Ocean and returned to Bristol on 6 August. The place where Cabot landed has never been definitively identified. Possible sites are Cape Breton Island, Newfoundland and southern Labrador. Cabot himself thought it was the north-east of Asia, which he claimed for England. Cabot reported to King Henry, who was delighted and made him a gift of £10. The explorer embarked on a second voyage, with five ships, in 1498. The fleet was lost at sea, though it is not known whether this was before or after he reached north America.

Below: Global view. Henry stands with Venetian sailor John Cabot, in a portrait from the Doges' Palace, Venice.

Above: White rose entwined with red when Elizabeth of York married the Lancastrian Henry Tudor (Henry VII) in 1486.

meet them, and at Stoke on 16 June the royalists defeated the rebel force and captured Simnel. Rebel leader John de la Pole, Earl of Lincoln, was killed. Backing for this uprising was never wholehearted among Yorkists. When Lincoln tried to raise support in Yorkshire he met with little success, and the gates of York were shut against him. King Henry felt that he could afford to be magnanimous and, rather than have Simnel executed, he gave him a job in the palace kitchens.

A second Pretender to the throne made more of an impact and proved a greater threat. Arriving in Ireland in 1491, an elegant and well-built young man from Flanders named Perkin Warbeck claimed to be Richard, Duke of York, the younger of the two princes in the Tower.

He won the support of various European rulers, including Charles VIII of France, Holy Roman Emperor Maximilian I and James IV, King of Scots, who awarded Warbeck a £1200 annual allowance and the hand of James's cousin, Lady Catherine Gordon. In 1497, Warbeck led an invasion of

England, landing in Cornwall with a small force and proclaiming himself King Richard IV. Marching inland, he did manage to gather some support but the revolt melted away in the face of an approaching royal army. Warbeck was captured and confessed himself to be an imposter. Henry cast him in the Tower alongside Edward, Earl of Warwick, but in 1499 had both men executed for plotting against the king.

Below: In Westminster Abbey a bronze tomb of 1518 by Italian Pietro Torrigiano commemorates Henry and Elizabeth.

THE TUDOR SUCCESSION
THE NEW DYNASTY, 1485–1509

 The future for the Tudor dynasty began to look brighter when, after nine months of marriage to King Henry, Elizabeth of York gave birth to a son at Winchester on 19 September 1486. Henry was keen to stress his Welsh-British rather than French-Plantagenet roots and named the boy Arthur after the legendary British king of the 5th century AD. At the age of three, Arthur was created Prince of Wales at Ludlow Castle on 29 November 1489. In the ceremony his father was praised as a restorer of Welsh pride, a King of all the Britons capable of bringing order after years of chaos.

A LOST PRINCE

Arthur was raised for kingship. He had the best education in literature and philosophy under the guidance of poet and chronicler Bernard André. At the age of 15 in 1501 he took control in his capacity as Prince of Wales of the council governing Wales. He made a significant diplomatic marriage to

Below: The great Dutch New Testament scholar Erasmus, a friend of Thomas More, was a visitor at the court of Henry VII.

QUEEN ELIZABETH'S CHILDREN

Queen Elizabeth gave birth to seven (or perhaps eight) children, but four died an untimely death, as did the queen herself. She died giving birth to her fourth daughter Katherine, on 2 Feb 1503. Her children were:

Arthur: Born 19 Sept 1486, died 2 April 1502
Margaret: Born 28 Nov 1489, died 18 Oct 1541
Henry: (the future King Henry VIII) Born 28 June 1491, died 28 Jan 1547
Elizabeth: Born 2 July 1492, died 14 Sept 1495
Mary: Born 18 March 1496, died 25 June 1533
Edmund: Born 21 Feb 1499, died 19 June 1500
Katherine: Born and died 2 Feb 1503

In some accounts another son named Edward was born, but most historians believe this name to be a mistaken form of Edmund.

Below: Three siblings. Arthur, Prince of Wales, with Prince Henry and Princess Margaret, aged 10, 5 and 7 in 1496.

Princess Catherine, the daughter of King Ferdinand of Aragon, on 14 November 1501, but the following year, on 2 April 1502, the prince died of consumption, leaving Catherine a widow at the age of 18 and leaving his brother Henry, Duke of York, heir to the throne.

DIPLOMATIC MARRIAGES

Henry VII had used the promise of Arthur's hand in marriage as a bargaining tool in diplomatic talks. Arthur and Catherine of Aragon had been promised to one another as early as 1488, when Arthur was 18 months old and Catherine was three. The plans for the wedding had then been reconfirmed in the Treaty of Medina del Campo, signed on 27 March 1489.

The importance of the Spanish alliance was reconfirmed when, just over a year after Arthur's death, it was agreed that Prince Henry, now aged 12, would marry Catherine of Aragon. In the event the wedding was postponed when

part of Catherine's agreed dowry was late to arrive. Prince Henry did not marry Catherine until after the death of his father Henry VII had made him King Henry VIII.

A second major diplomatic marriage was arranged with Scotland in a treaty of perpetual peace signed by English and Scottish diplomats in London, in 1502. At Holyrood House palace, Edinburgh, on 8 August 1503, King James IV of Scots married Henry VII's daughter Margaret Tudor. Scots poet William Dunbar produced a poem, 'The Thistle and the Rose', to celebrate the rapprochement between the ruling houses of Scotland and England.

A PALACE IN RICHMOND

The royal palace at Sheen in Surrey was Henry VII's favourite residence, and princes Arthur and Henry were raised there. At Christmas in 1497, however, Sheen Palace burned to the ground after a conflagration began in the king's quarters. Henry ordered the construction of a magnificent new dwelling and renamed the site Richmond after his family's earldom in Yorkshire.

Completed in 1501, Henry called the new palace, 'this earthly paradise of our realm of England'. It had four towers and a great timber-roofed hall 100ft (70m) in length.

Henry's court was a place of great culture, where leading names of European learning such as the humanists Polydore Vergil and Desiderius Erasmus were welcomed. Vergil arrived in England in 1502 and served as Archdeacon of Wells; his *Anglicae Historiae Libri XXVI* (1534–55) is a valued resource for historians studying Henry VII's reign. Erasmus was a friend and frequent guest of Thomas More – a great name of Henry VIII's reign – who was already active at court in Henry VII's time, serving as a royal envoy to

Above: In 1499 Sheen Palace at Richard burnt down; it was rebuilt by Henry VII.

Flanders. Henry rewarded acclaimed Scots poet William Dunbar for his poem in praise of London in 1501. He also began work on a magnificent new chapel at Westminster Abbey, which he hoped to dedicate to Henry VI.

A REIGN OF MANY ADVANCES

Henry died at Richmond, aged 52, after a reign of 23 years. His reign must be judged a significant success. He created stability after decades of civil dissension, thereby establishing the Tudor dynasty while, through astute diplomacy, he boosted England's standing in Europe and stabilized the country's finances.

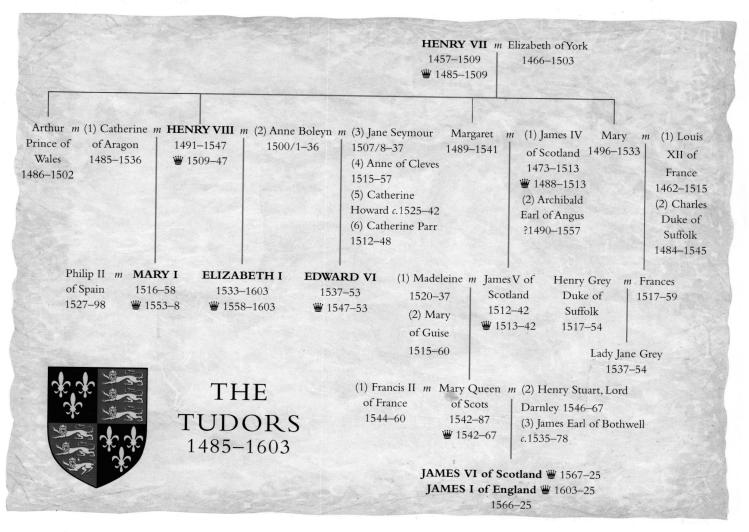

HENRY VII *m* Elizabeth of York
1457–1509   1466–1503
♛ 1485–1509

| Arthur *m* (1) Catherine *m* | **HENRY VIII** *m* (2) Anne Boleyn *m* (3) Jane Seymour | Margaret *m* (1) James IV | Mary *m* (1) Louis |

Arthur *m* (1) Catherine *m* **HENRY VIII** *m* (2) Anne Boleyn *m* (3) Jane Seymour
Prince of   of Aragon   1491–1547   1500/1–36   1507/8–37
Wales   1485–1536   ♛ 1509–47   (4) Anne of Cleves
1486–1502   1515–57
                              (5) Catherine
                              Howard *c.*1525–42
                              (6) Catherine Parr
                              1512–48

Margaret *m* (1) James IV
1489–1541   of Scotland
             1473–1513
             ♛ 1488–1513
             (2) Archibald
             Earl of Angus
             ?1490–1557

Mary *m* (1) Louis
1496–1533   XII of
          France
          1462–1515
          (2) Charles
          Duke of
          Suffolk
          1484–1545

Philip II *m* **MARY I**
of Spain   1516–58
1527–98   ♛ 1553–8

ELIZABETH I
1533–1603
♛ 1558–1603

EDWARD VI
1537–53
♛ 1547–53

(1) Madeleine *m* James V of
1520–37   Scotland
(2) Mary   1512–42
of Guise   ♛ 1513–42
1515–60

Henry Grey *m* Frances
Duke of   1517–59
Suffolk
1517–54

Lady Jane Grey
1537–54

THE TUDORS
1485–1603

(1) Francis II *m* Mary Queen *m* (2) Henry Stuart, Lord
of France   of Scots   Darnley 1546–67
1544–60   1542–87   (3) James Earl of Bothwell
         ♛ 1542–67   *c.*1535–78

JAMES VI of Scotland ♛ 1567–25
JAMES I of England ♛ 1603–25
1566–25

HENRY VIII

1509–1547

 Henry VIII acceded to the throne aged 17, a young man of imposing build and looks, 6ft 3in (1.9m) tall, with red hair and a florid complexion, full of youthful exuberance and with a love of display and extravagant pleasures. In character and appearance, the new king presented a marked contrast to his cautious and sober-faced father, who in the last years of his reign had been stricken with tuberculosis.

HONOURING THE FATHER

In the first month of his reign, Henry honoured the memory of Henry VII, presiding over a long and splendid funeral procession and memorial service as the late king's body was carried to Westminster from Richmond, where he had died, and interred in the Abbey.

Henry VII was buried there on 11 May 1509. The magnificent chapel that the late king had begun in 1503 and hoped to dedicate to Henry VI became his own final resting place and a monument to the glories of the Tudor dynasty. A magnificent marble and gilt bronze tomb effigy of Henry VII and his beloved queen, Elizabeth, by the Florentine sculptor Pietro Torrigiano, was completed in 1518.

Within two months of his accession, Henry married his brother Arthur's widow, Catherine of Aragon, in accordance with a diplomatic agreement of 1503 and, so the young king said, in honour of his father's dying wish. The marriage in the Church of the Franciscans, at Greenwich on 11 June, was followed by a joint coronation in Westminster Abbey on 24 June. A huge

Above: Cardinal Wolsey dominated Henry VIII's government, 1515–29. He had great self-belief and enormous reserves of energy.

HENRY VIII, KING OF ENGLAND, 1509–1547

Birth: 28 June 1491, Greenwich Palace
Father: Henry VII
Mother: Elizabeth of York
Accession: 21 April 1509
Coronation: 24 June 1509, Westminster Abbey
Queens: Catherine of Aragon (m. 11 June 1509; d. 1536); Anne Boleyn (m. 24 Jan 1533; executed 19 May 1536); Jane Seymour (m. 30 May 1536; d. 24 Oct 1537); Anne of Cleves (m. 6 Jan 1540; d. 17 July 1557); Catherine Howard (m. 28 July 1540; executed 13 Feb 1542); Catherine Parr (m. 12 Jul 1543; d. 7 Sept 1548).
Succeeded by: His son, Edward VI, aged 9
Greatest achievement: Introducing the Protestant Reformation to England
16 Aug 1513: Defeats French at the Battle of the Spurs
20 Feb 1516: Birth of the future Queen Mary I

Above: With a small mouth and wide face, Henry resembled Edward IV.

1518: Treaty of London: mutual defence pact between England, Spain, France and the Holy Roman Empire

7–24 June 1520: Summit with Francis I of France at 'Field of the Cloth of Gold'
23 May 1533: Marriage to Catherine of Aragon annulled
1 June 1533: Anne Boleyn crowned Queen
7 Sept 1533: Birth of the future Queen Elizabeth I
30 Apr 1534: Act of Succession declares Princess Mary illegitimate and make Princess Elizabeth heir to throne
28 Nov 1534: Act of Supremacy makes Henry 'Supreme Head' of the Church of England
19 May 1536: Anne Boleyn executed
12 Oct 1537: Queen Jane Seymour gives birth to future Edward VI
1539: Publication of the 'Great Bible' in English
1541: Henry declares himself 'King of Ireland'
13 Feb 1542: Catherine Howard executed
Death: 28 Jan 1547, Whitehall Palace

banquet in Westminster Hall was capped by a week of ceremonial jousting to mark the occasion.

INTERNATIONAL DIPLOMACY

Henry VII had won England a significant place in Europe through marriage and diplomatic alliance and, in the first years of his reign, King Henry VIII determined to cement this international standing. His marriage to his brother's widow, Catherine, in 1509 cemented the alliance with the Spanish kingdom of Aragon against France. In 1511 the Holy Roman Emperor, Maximilian, made Henry a gift of a suit of the best armour in Europe, from Germany, in honour of the young king's prowess in jousting at tournaments.

In 1512 Henry set out to emulate his great predecessor Henry V by reconquering France. He won the support of Pope Julius II and, after forming an alliance with his father-in-law Ferdinand of Aragon and the Holy Roman Emperor Maximilian, declared war in April 1512 and sent an English army to Gascony. This expedition ended in mutiny and failure. The next year led

Below: Cardinal Wolsey began the building of Hampton Court Palace in 1515. Henry took it over when Wolsey fell from favour.

'GREAT HARRY'

At more than 1000 tons in weight, with five masts and five tiers of guns, the *Henri Grace à Dieu* – or 'Great Harry', as she was more popularly known – was the world's largest battleship when she was launched at Erith on 13 June 1514. Henry was a great believer in the need for English sea power to protect merchant vessels and back up land armies in European conflicts. Unfortunately, the 'Great Harry' only just survived its namesake: six years after Henry VIII's death in 1547, the warship was accidentally destroyed in a fire in 1553.

Above: 'Great Harry' *was among the first ships to carry guns fired through side-ports.*

to a more successful invasion of France from Calais. On 16 August 1513 Henry won the Battle of the Spurs, so called because the French fled without joining battle and suffered the indignity of the capture of several standards and important prisoners. The allied army also captured the towns of Thérouanne and Tournai. At home, meanwhile, an attempted invasion by King James IV of Scots met with disaster. His army was annihilated by an English force under the 70-year-old Earl of Surrey at Flodden, Northumberland, and James IV himself was killed.

Henry's chief adviser Thomas Wolsey pressed for peace with France, for the war there was achieving little but costing a great deal. A treaty was agreed on 6 August 1514 under which Henry VIII's 17-year-old sister, Mary Tudor, married France's 52-year-old king, Louis XII. This was the first marriage between French and English royals since Henry V's match with Catharine of Valois a century earlier. An unexpected alliance with France was complemented by the four-way Treaty of London of 1518 under which Spain, France, England and the Holy Roman Empire agreed a mutual defence pact.

Such was Henry's European standing that in 1519, with papal encouragement, he even manoeuvred to try to win election as Holy Roman Emperor following Maximilian's death. However, the electors in Frankfurt preferred the claim of King Charles of Spain.

The most extraordinary statement of England's new international standing in the early 16th century was the sumptuous three-week summit with France held near Calais in June 1520. Stage-managed by Thomas Wolsey and known as the 'Field of the Cloth of Gold', the event comprised a series of meetings between Henry and King Francis I of France accompanied by banquets, jousting, hunting and courtly entertainments.

THE SIX WIVES OF HENRY VIII
ROYAL MARRIAGES, 1509–1547

Within two months of his accession to the throne, Henry married his brother Arthur's widow, Catherine of Aragon. Catherine was certainly a suitable bride for the young prince. Although she had been married to his brother, she was only five years older than the 18-year-old Henry and was widely considered a beauty. She was the daughter of King Ferdinand of Aragon and Queen Isabella of Castile and the aunt of Europe's most powerful royal, Charles, Duke of Burgundy, King of Spain and future Holy Roman Emperor. Catherine was very well educated; she was fluent in Latin, French and her native Spanish, although she found it less easy to speak in English.

DESPERATE FOR AN HEIR

Catherine was, however, unable to provide what Henry, determined to safeguard the Tudor dynasty, was desperate to have: a healthy baby boy as his heir. She gave birth to a stillborn daughter in 1510, then in 1511 to a son,

Below: Catherine of Aragon. Highly intelligent, she was an effective regent when Henry fought in France 1512–14.

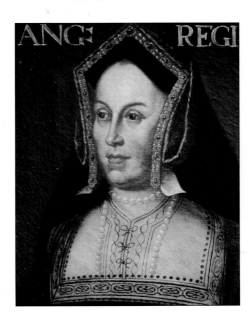

Above: Anne Boleyn. Although she failed to provide a male heir, she did give birth to the baby destined for glory as Elizabeth I.

christened Henry, who tragically died aged two months. Another son, born in November 1513, died after only a few hours' life and a third son was stillborn in December 1514. Finally on 18 February 1516 a healthy baby daughter, later christened Mary, was born. The next child, born in November 1518, was a stillborn daughter.

Henry meanwhile maintained an active sexual life with his mistresses, one of whom, Elizabeth Blount, gave birth to a healthy boy, named Henry Fitzroy, in 1519. This served to convince the king of his reproductive virility and focused his mind on the need for a legitimate male heir. Matters came to a head in 1527 when Henry, infatuated with court beauty Anne Boleyn, declared that his marriage to Catherine of Aragon had never been legitimate since she was his brother Arthur's wife before she became Henry's bride.

'ANNE OF A THOUSAND DAYS'

The daughter of Sir Thomas Boleyn, Anne was dark-haired, with beautiful features, a long graceful neck and lively

Above: Jane Seymour. She was lady in waiting to both Catherine of Aragon and Anne Boleyn before marrying the king.

manners. She was sister of one of Henry's mistresses, Mary, but despite lavish gifts of jewellery from the king, she refused to become his mistress and held out for becoming his queen. At court she was unpopular and gossip suggested she must be a witch to have driven the king to such desperation.

Henry began proceedings to have his marriage to Catherine declared invalid, but Pope Clement VII – who was under pressure from Catherine's nephew, Charles V of Spain – would not grant the annulment. After almost six years, Henry finally had his way when he secretly married Anne Boleyn on 24 January 1533.

On 23 May Thomas Cranmer, the Archbishop of Canterbury, declared the king's first marriage invalid. Anne was crowned queen on 1 June, and the following month Catherine of Aragon, who refused to renounce her own regal title, was placed under house arrest at Buckden, Cambridgeshire. On 7 September 1533, at Greenwich, Anne gave birth to a daughter, the future Queen Elizabeth I.

Above: Anne of Cleves. After accepting an annulment of her marriage to Henry, she lived on for 17 years until 1557.

Anne's elevation was short-lived. She, too, failed to provide a healthy male heir and the king's interest turned to one of Anne's ladies in waiting, Jane Seymour. After Anne had a miscarriage and then gave birth to a stillborn baby boy, Henry accused her – probably falsely – of adultery and on 2 May 1536 cast her into the Tower of London.

Anne was unanimously convicted by a court of peers under her uncle the Duke of Norfolk and beheaded on 19 May 1536. She kept her wits to the last, declaring, 'The king has been good to me. He promoted me from a simple maid to a marchioness. Then he raised me to be a queen. Now he will raise me to be a martyr'.

NO LONGER A LADY-IN-WAITING
The very next day, Henry proposed to Jane Seymour and the couple were married before the month was out, on 30 May in Whitehall Palace.

A modest woman with a child-like face, Jane was well-liked at court and finally delivered what the king and the country longed for: a legitimate male heir. Prince Edward was born on 12 October 1537 at Hampton Court Palace.

However, twelve days later Jane died suddenly, perhaps from post-natal fever, causing her royal husband apparently genuine grief.

THE 'FLANDERS MARE'
Henry's fourth wedding was a diplomatic match with Princess Anne of Cleves, sister of William, Duke of Cleves in Germany, made to cement an alliance with Protestant German princes against the Holy Roman Emperor Charles V.

Henry was not pleased when he set eyes on his rather plain-looking bride, and declared to Thomas Cromwell, 'My lord, if it were not to satisfy the world and my realm, I would not do that I must this day for none earthly thing'.

Nevertheless, the wedding went ahead at Greenwich Palace on 6 January 1540. By all accounts Henry's marriage to the woman he called his 'Flanders mare' was never consummated, and Henry was apparently humiliated and angered by his impotence.

In summer 1540 the queen agreed happily to a divorce that freed Henry to marry the woman who had become the object of his latest infatuation, the ill-fated Catherine Howard.

Below: Catherine Parr. Well educated and religious, she wrote A Lamentacion or Complaynt of a Sinner *in 1548.*

Above: Catherine Howard. A cousin of Anne Boleyn, she served as a maid of honour to Anne of Cleves.

A WOMAN OF EXPERIENCE
Beautiful, buxom and with healthy appetites, Catherine was one of ten children of the impoverished Lord Edmund Howard. She married Henry on 28 July 1540, less than three weeks after the king's fourth marriage to Anne of Cleves had been annulled on 9 July. Catherine's downfall came when Henry discovered that she had had premarital affairs and may even had been unfaithful after her marriage to the king. With the backing of a parliamentary bill declaring it treason for an 'unchaste' woman to wed a king, Catherine was beheaded at the Tower of London on 13 February 1542.

A COMPANION IN OLD AGE
Henry wed his sixth wife, Catherine Parr, at Hampton Court on 12 July 1543. She had already been twice married and twice widowed. An intelligent and well-balanced woman, she was a helpful companion for Henry in his last years. She was a good stepmother to the three surviving children of his previous marriages and oversaw their education. She survived the king and took a fourth husband, Lord Thomas Seymour.

HENRY AND THE CHURCH OF ENGLAND
DEFENDER OF THE FAITH, 1529–1547

Henry VIII's momentous religious reforms were driven by self-interest: the king's increasingly desperate desire to rid himself of Catherine of Aragon so that he could wed Anne Boleyn.

Henry instructed Thomas Wolsey, the dominant statesman of the first part of the reign, to use his influence as papal legate to persuade Pope Clement VII to grant an annulment of the marriage. Wolsey failed: a legatine court in London examining the validity of King

Below: Royal palaces, major towns and the spread of monasteries in the early years of Henry VIII's reign. The Dissolution of the Monasteries began in 1536.

Henry's case for divorce and presided over by Wolsey and Cardinal Campeggio in May–July 1529 adjourned without reaching a decision, and on 13 July the same year Pope Clement VII ordered that the case must be heard in Rome.

HEAD OF THE CHURCH

Henry turned on Wolsey. A broken man, the king's former adviser died before he could be thrown in the Tower. Henry forced the Convocations of the English clergy at York and Canterbury to submit to him on two issues. In February 1531 they recognized him as 'Supreme Head of the Church of England' and in May 1532

Above: Cranmer, the first Protestant Archbishop of Canterbury, freed Henry to wed Anne Boleyn when he declared the marriage to Catherine of Aragon invalid.

they accepted that all their legislation was subject to royal approval. The king rather than the pope was the final authority on church matters.

Henry, while remaining a Catholic, was convinced of the rightness of his case, so much so that he travelled to a diplomatic summit with the King of France in October–November 1532 with Anne Boleyn as his consort.

Thomas Cranmer, appointed Archbishop of Canterbury on 30 March 1533, won the backing of the Convocation of English clergy to the twin propositions that, first, the Bible outlawed a man's marriage to his brother's widow and, second, that the pope had no authority to allow such a union. Archbishop Cranmer declared the marriage to Catherine invalid on 23 May 1533 and Henry had Anne Boleyn crowned as Queen on 1 June. By this time Anne was already six months pregnant.

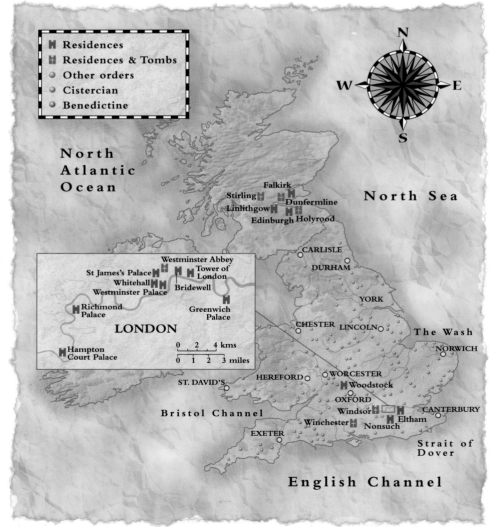

Map legend:
- Residences
- Residences & Tombs
- Other orders
- Cistercian
- Benedictine

North Atlantic Ocean

North Sea

Falkirk
Stirling
Linlithgow
Dunfermline
Edinburgh Holyrood

CARLISLE
DURHAM
YORK
CHESTER LINCOLN
The Wash
NORWICH
WORCESTER
HEREFORD
Woodstock
OXFORD
Windsor
CANTERBURY
Winchester
Eltham
Nonsuch
EXETER
ST. DAVID'S

Bristol Channel

Strait of Dover

English Channel

London inset:
Westminster Abbey
St James's Palace
Whitehall
Westminster Palace
Tower of London
Bridewell
Richmond Palace
Greenwich Palace
LONDON
Hampton Court Palace
0 2 4 kms
0 1 2 3 miles

TIDE OF CHANGE

Both Cranmer and Henry's Chancellor, Thomas Cromwell, were sympathetic to what contemporaries called the 'new learning' of the Reformed (Protestant) Church, and they were happy to engineer Henry's extinction of papal authority in England.

The Act of Succession, passed by Parliament on 30 April 1534, provided legal backing to Cranmer's May 1533 declaration. Under the Act, the marriage to Catherine of Aragon was annulled, making Catherine's daughter, Mary, illegitimate, while every adult male was required to take a succession oath of allegiance to Queen Anne that recognized her daughter Elizabeth and any other possible children of the marriage as heirs to the throne.

Above: The medieval Glastonbury Abbey was one of those broken up in the Dissolution of the Monasteries.

Above: The frontispiece to the 1539 Great Bible in English shows Henry giving the 'Word of God' to Cranmer and Cromwell.

Under the Act of Supremacy, passed by Parliament on 28 November 1534, Henry VIII was declared, 'The only supreme head in earth of the Church of England'. Further legislation made it treasonable to deny his supremacy. Under this law the former Chancellor Thomas More and Bishop John Fisher of Rochester were executed in 1535.

SQUANDERED WEALTH

As the head of the Church in England, Henry now had access to its vast landholdings. The Dissolution of the Monasteries, which was implemented by Cromwell in 1536–40, brought immense wealth to the crown, most of which Henry squandered. The last monastery to be dissolved was Waltham Abbey in March 1540.

Throughout the years to 1540, Cromwell and Cranmer moved on the religious revolution in England – with a 1538 campaign in which the country's major shrines were closed down, and injunctions in 1536 and 1538 making use of the English-language Bible compulsory in all English parishes.

Below: Victim of the Reformation. This dramatic vision of Thomas More's fall is by French artist Antoine Caron (1521–99).

AA DEBATE FOR SCHOLARS

The debate over whether King Henry had Biblical justification for divorcing Queen Catherine exercised scholars across Europe for a decade.

The two key Biblical texts were Leviticus Chapter 20 Verse 21: 'If a man shall take his brother's wife, it is an impurity; he hath uncovered his brother's nakedness; they shall be childless' and Deuteronomy Chapter 25 Verse 5: 'When brethren dwell together and one of them dieth without children, the wife of the deceased shall not marry to another: but his brother shall take her, and raise up seed for his brother'.

While Henry could claim, citing Leviticus, that his marriage was accursed under Biblical law and that this was the reason for the trouble Catherine had had in bearing a healthy son, Catherine's defenders could argue, with the backing of Deuteronomy, that it had been Henry's duty to marry her. Moreover, Catherine argued that her marriage to Arthur had never been consummated and so the issue did not even arise.

THE LAST YEARS OF HENRY VIII
DEATH OF A MONARCH, 1536–1547

The religious changes of the mid-1530s was to provoke the worst rebellion faced by any Tudor ruler and the most serious civil unrest since the Peasants' Revolt of 1381. A major Catholic uprising across the north of England in 1536 called on the king to make peace with the pope, to reopen the monasteries that had been closed, to restore Princess Mary as heir to the throne and to exclude low-born councillors from his inner circle; a reference to the widely unpopular Thomas Cromwell, Thomas Cranmer and Hugh Latimer. The rebels, who gathered under the badge of the 'Five Wounds of Christ' and who called themselves the 'Pilgrimage of Grace for the Commonweal', even reopened some of the monasteries that had been closed. Their leader was a Yorkshire lawyer named Robert Aske.

The crisis was averted. Henry's representative, Thomas Howard, the Duke of Norfolk, managed to disperse the uprising by promising a general amnesty and a Parliament in York within twelve months. That might have been that, but in January 1537, Yorkshire landowner Sir Francis Bigod tried to

Left: Thomas Cromwell. He died in great agony on Tower Hill on 28 July 1540 because the executioner's axe was blunt.

Above: Unique glory. Henry VIII's Nonsuch Palace in Surrey was so called because there was 'none such' (none like it). He died before the palace was complete.

start a separate and entirely different revolt. The leaders of the Pilgrimage of Grace, including Aske, were arrested, given an arbitrary trial and executed in a brutal show of royal authority in June 1537.

AN ENGLISH 'EMPIRE'

The year 1536 saw the first of two major Acts of Parliament under which Wales became part of the kingdom of England and Wales. The 1536 Act stated, 'Wales is and ever has been incorporated, annexed, united and subject to and under the imperial Crown of the Realm as a member of the same'. In this and a second Act of 1543, Wales was organized into 13 counties, each represented by MPs at the Westminster Parliament, and the Welsh language was banned for official use. Those who spoke only Welsh were barred from public office.

In 1541 the Irish Parliament accepted Henry as King of Ireland and Head of the Irish Church. Under the Crown of Ireland Act, the king of England became automatically the king of Ireland.

Henry was the first to hold this title; previous Irish rulers had been 'high kings' or 'Lord of Ireland', a title which was bestowed on Henry II by the pope. Henry VIII had no desire to rule Ireland by right of a title granted by the papacy before the Reformation.

Henry's attempt to bring Scotland into the English kingdom met with less success. The Treaty of Greenwich, in 1543, proposed a dynastic alliance in which Henry's seven-year-old heir, Prince Edward, would marry Mary, Queen of Scots, then less than one year old. However, a change of heart by Scots governor the Earl of Arran provoked Henry to unleash a military raid commanded by Edward Seymour, Earl of Hertford in 1544.

The Earl of Hertford captured Leith and Edinburgh, where he started fires that reportedly burned for four days, in a campaign dubbed 'rough wooing' because of the earlier marriage negotiations. However, the invasion had no lasting impact. In February the following year the English force was defeated by Scottish troops at the battle of Ancrum Moor.

The latter years of the reign saw England at war with Scotland, France and Ireland, These were ruinously expensive campaigns and in order to pay for them Henry was forced to sell on into private ownership the greater part of the lands he had seized from the Church in the Dissolution of the Monasteries.

THE FALL OF CROMWELL

Henry's chief minister Thomas Cromwell fell abruptly from power in the summer of 1540, when his opponents at court, notably Thomas Howard, third Duke of Norfolk and Bishop Stephen Gardiner, persuaded the king that Cromwell was guilty of heresy and of plotting treason.

Historians generally agree that Cromwell's fall from the king's grace was mainly due to the disaster of Henry's marriage to Anne of Cleves, which Cromwell had negotiated as a diplomatic match in the autumn of 1539. The wedding took place in January 1540, but the match was apparently never consummated and, although Cromwell was elevated to the earldom of Essex as late as April 1540, he never recovered the king's favour. As a result of Norfolk's machinations, Cromwell was arrested in the king's council chamber on 10 June 1540, convicted without trial and beheaded.

CORRUPTION OF THE BODY

In the mid-1540s Henry became grossly corpulent and prematurely aged. Unable to exercise after a sporting injury to his leg, he continued to indulge his vast appetite and his waistline grew to 66in (1.68m). He could no longer walk, but had to be carried by four courtiers; he began to lose his hair and was feared at court for the ease with which he lost his temper. But his sixth wife, Catherine Parr, was attentive to his needs and brought him some peace.

Nevertheless the king fell into a long illness and the end of his reign was obviously drawing near. The Conservative-Catholic faction led by the Duke of Norfolk manoeuvred against supporters of the reformed religion for influence over the country's future direction. The matter was decided by the downfall of the Duke of Norfolk's family. Norfolk's son Henry Howard, Earl of Surrey, bragged of his family's Plantagenet ancestry – as descendants of Edward III – and added the royal arms to his heraldic device. Surrey was found guilty of treason and beheaded on 19 January 1547. His father was condemned without trial as

Above: His Majesty. The words, associated with the Roman emperor, were first used of the king in 1534 as he sought to establish his authority to challenge the pope.

a traitor and was scheduled to be executed on the very day that the king happened to die.

Henry's reign – which had seen such momentous changes in State and Church – ended early in the morning of 28 January 1547. Despite six marriages and all the desperate manoeuvring to ensure a succession, the king was survived by only three legitimate children, including his sole male heir, the nine-year-old Prince Edward.

EDWARD VI
1547–1553

Edward was a small, pale, precocious boy aged nine when he acceded to the throne previously occupied by his giant of a father. The boy-king was already highly educated, having learned Latin and Greek from the age of five, and well versed in Protestant ideas after studying northern Europe's religious 'reformation'. He was serious and rather withdrawn, for he had little experience of family life until the kindness of Queen Catherine Parr brought Henry's three children together after 1544. His pastimes were solitary: viewing the night sky and playing the lute.

THE LORD PROTECTOR

On 18 February, King Edward processed from the Tower of London to Westminster Abbey. He wore a magnificent outfit of cloth of silver and white velvet and rode beneath a crimson canopy on a white charger. Much to his delight, street entertainments were laid on along the route, including a high-wire act at St Paul's, an 'angel' at Cheapside, a children's choir at Cornhill and a 'giant' at London Bridge. The following day he was crowned in the Abbey, amid solemn ceremonial.

His country was in the hands of his uncle Edward Seymour, Earl of Hertford. King Henry had stipulated in

Above: Prince precocious. Edward was known throughout Europe for his learning and intelligence, and also for his saintly piety.

his will the creation of a ruling regency council. However, Seymour had been able to delay public announcement of King Henry's death for three days until 31 January, while he manoeuvred behind the scenes to have himself declared Lord Protector. Subsequently he broke up the council of regents and assumed sole power. On 16 February he was named Duke of Somerset.

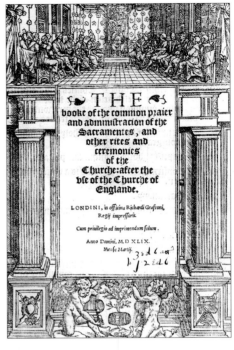

Above: The frontispiece of the 1549 Book of Common Prayer shows the young King Edward (top) sitting in council.

The Protector maintained Henry's wars against France and Scotland. After initial difficulties he won a significant victory at the Battle of Pinkie near Musselburgh, Scotland, on 10 September 1547 but was unable to build on it. The Scots aligned themselves with the French, who besieged Boulogne, which England had taken under a 1546 treaty.

Somerset was committed to the Protestant cause and under his Protectorate strict religious reforms were put in place. The 1549 Act of Uniformity outlawed the traditional Catholic Mass and made the use of the Book of Common Prayer compulsory.

ROYAL LOVE TRIANGLE

Early in 1549 one of the king's uncles, Lord Thomas Seymour, was executed after an extraordinary royal love scandal. Seymour, brother of Henry VIII's favourite wife, Jane Seymour, secretly

---

EDWARD VI, KING OF ENGLAND, 1547–1553

Birth: 12 Oct 1537, Hampton Court
Father: Henry VIII
Mother: Jane Seymour
Accession: 28 Jan 1547
Coronation: 20 Feb 1547, Westminster Abbey
Succeeded by: His cousin Lady Jane Grey, for nine days; afterwards by his sister, Mary I
Greatest achievement: Foundation of

grammar schools in several towns
10 Sept 1547: Battle of Pinkie
1549: First Book of Common Prayer. Popular protests against the new prayer book and land enclosures
Oct 1549: John Dudley, Earl of Warwick, replaces Edward Seymour, Duke of Somerset, as Lord Protector
1552: Second Book of Common Prayer
Death: 6 July 1553, London

married Henry's widow Catherine Parr in the very year of the king's death. Then reports circulated that he had been caught trying to seduce Henry's daughter, the red-haired Princess Elizabeth. Some versions indicated that a love triangle had developed involving Catherine, Thomas and Elizabeth and that he had even fathered a child with Elizabeth. Lord Thomas was charged with high treason and the fact that his brother, Edward, was Lord Protector did not save him. He was executed on 20 March 1549.

By the summer of 1549 the Duke of Somerset's hold on power was looking insecure. Catholics in the West Country rose up against the imposition of the Book of Common Prayer, while peasants in Norfolk, the Midlands and Yorkshire protested against land enclosures by local gentry. John Dudley, Earl of Warwick, led troops against the rebels at Dussindale in Norfolk on 26 August, and in the ensuing massacre at least 3,500 people were killed.

Among aristocrats at court and in London, Somerset came under concerted attack for his stated sympathy with the peasant opponents of land enclosure. Warwick saw his chance to seize power and in October had Somerset arrested and thrown in the Tower of London, while he himself was declared Lord Protector in his place.

THE KING'S SICKNESS

Warwick, created the Earl of Northumberland in 1551, oversaw the imposition of a stricter form of Protestant worship in 1552 with a second Book of Common Prayer and a new measure outlawing Catholic dress and forms of worship, including priestly vestments and prayers for the dead.

By the autumn and winter of that year it was clear that the young king was sickening unto death and the most pressing matter for Protestants such as Northumberland became finding a way of preventing a Catholic succession to the throne.

King Edward had fallen ill in summer 1552 and was diagnosed with smallpox and measles, but he did not recover and apparently developed pulmonary tuberculosis in the very cold winter that followed. He was also losing

Above: Sir Edward Seymour, Duke of Somerset and Lord Protector, was also a great military commander, victor both at Pinkie (1544) and Boulogne (1545).

his hair and, according to some accounts had inherited congenital syphilis from his father. Henry VIII's will stated that if Edward died childless, the throne would pass to Edward's sisters, first Mary then Elizabeth. Mary, next in line, was a Catholic and would not only undo hard-won Protestant reforms but also move against Northumberland himself.

As Edward VI neared death, he and Northumberland drew up a 'device' – a kind of will – that shut Mary and Elizabeth out from the succession, and named Lady Jane Grey as his heir.

Lady Jane, the 16-year-old daughter of the Duke of Suffolk, was Henry VIII's great-niece, for her mother Frances was the daughter of Henry VIII's sister Mary. Most importantly for those planning her succession, she was a devout Protestant.

The king's council and Parliament accepted the device. Edward VI died in London on 6 July 1553 and four days later Lady Jane Grey was declared Queen by the King's Council.

Left: The English painting An Allegory of the Reformation *(c. 1570) shows the pope and his cronies undone by Edward.*

MARY I
1553–1558

The Earl of Northumberland's attempt to engineer the succession in favour of his niece, Lady Jane Grey, was nothing more than a total failure. Henry VIII's eldest daughter and his rightful heir, Mary Tudor, proclaimed herself queen on 19 July 1553 and was welcomed to the capital by cheering crowds on 3 August.

Below: The Tudor Princess. This portrait, by 'Master John', shows the future queen as a young woman of 28, in 1544.

RETURN TO CATHOLICISM

Mary was an intelligent and independent-minded woman with a fierce devotion to the Roman Catholic faith, which her father Henry VIII had sought to undermine. Now, as queen, she set about eradicating Protestantism.

By mid-September she had arrested the most important Protestant clerics, including the Archbishop of Canterbury Thomas Cranmer, principal author of the Books of Common Prayer published in 1549 and 1552 and architect of many of Edward VI's reforms.

Acts of Parliament rapidly repealed the anti-Catholic legislation introduced under Edward. On 16 November, moreover, she declared her intention of marrying the Roman Catholic Prince Philip of Spain, son of Charles V, Holy Roman Emperor and King of Spain. It was increasingly clear that Mary intended to sweep away the Church of England and return her country to full-blown European Catholicism. The proposed marriage, meanwhile, raised the unwelcome possibility that England would become no more than a satellite

ANNO DNI · 1544

LADI MARI THE MOST KINGE HENRI

DOVGHTER TO VERTVOVS PRINCE THE EIGHT

THE AGE OF · XXVIII YERES ·

MARY I, QUEEN OF ENGLAND, 1553–1558

Birth: 18 Feb 1516, Greenwich Palace

Father: Henry VIII

Mother: Catherine of Aragon

Accession: 19 July 1553

Coronation: 1 Oct 1553, Westminster Abbey

Husband: Philip II of Spain, son of Charles V, King of Spain and Holy Roman Emperor (m. 25 July 1554; d. 1598)

Succeeded by: Her sister Elizabeth I

Greatest achievement: England's first reigning queen

25 Jan 1554: Kentish rebels attack London

30 Nov 1554: Cardinal Reginald Pole absolves England following dispute with papacy

Aug 1555: King Philip abandons Mary and leaves for Netherlands

16 Oct 1555: Bishops Hugh Latimer and Nicholas Ridley martyred

21 March 1556: Archbishop of Canterbury, Thomas Cranmer, martyred

7 Jan 1558: French retake Calais

Death: 17 Nov 1558, London

QUEEN FOR NINE DAYS

The beautiful, learned, sensitive and intelligent 15-year-old Lady Jane Grey is said to have fainted when the idea was first put to her that she should become queen. In the end she reluctantly permitted Edward and her uncle, Northumberland, to elevate her to the English crown. She married Northumberland's son, Lord Guildford Dudley, on 21 May 1553. Northumberland proclaimed her queen on 10 July and urged her to name his son king, but she steadfastly refused. In the event, she ruled for just nine days before she was deposed by the rightful heir, Mary.

Lady Jane and her husband were thrown in the Tower of London in July 1553 and executed on 12 February 1554.

Right: In 1833 Paul Delaroche painted Lady Jane Grey as an innocent victim.

Above: A Protestant cartoon celebrates the martyrdom of Hugh Latimer, Nicholas Ridley and Thomas Cranmer.

territory of Spain. Rebellion erupted: on 25 January, Sir Thomas Wyatt marched to London at the head of a troop of Kentish rebels to protest against the planned Spanish marriage.

As 7,000-odd rebels prepared to attack the City of London, Queen Mary made a passionate appeal to an assembly of Londoners declaring, 'I love you as a mother loves her child'. She won their loyalty and the rebels were crushed.

Wyatt was executed on 11 April and Mary's sister Princess Elizabeth, who was suspected of involvement in the plot, was cast into the Tower of London and only freed after a period of two months' imprisonment.

Opposition to the marriage remained strong, and broadsheets and ballads opposing the match were all the rage in London. The wedding went ahead, however. Mary, 38, married Philip – at 27, eleven years her junior – on 25 July 1554 in Winchester Cathedral. Philip was proclaimed King of England, but only in the role of king-consort. He would not succeed to the throne if the marriage were childless.

BLOODY MARY

On 20 November 1554 papal legate Cardinal Reginald Pole, exiled since 1532 in protest at Henry VIII's religious reforms, returned to England. Ten days later, Pole pronounced absolution marking England's formal peace with the pope. The following year began the execution of Protestants that earned the queen her reputation in English history as 'Bloody Mary'. In all, 287 Protestants were slain at her command.

On 16 October 1555, Bishops Hugh Latimer and Nicholas Ridley were burned at the stake while Thomas Cranmer watched from his prison cell; Latimer sounded a resounding note as he comforted his fellow victim. 'We shall this day light such a candle by God's grace in England as I trust shall never be put out'.

Mary's marriage, meanwhile, proved unhappy. The queen was deeply in love with her husband, but he did not reciprocate her feelings. In 1555 Mary suffered a phantom pregnancy, which raised and then dashed hopes that an heir might be born. The same month she was abandoned by her consort, as Philip left for the Netherlands. He did not return until July 1557, despite much anguished pleading from Mary. Even then, Philip's main motive in returning was to persuade Mary to ally England with Spain in a war against France.

Within a few months he departed once again for the Netherlands. The war with France into which he had drawn her was a disaster, resulting in the loss to French troops of Calais, England's last French possession. This deeply affected Mary, who declared, 'When I have died and am opened up, you will find Calais lying in my heart'.

On 17 November 1558 Mary died at St James's Palace, tortured by the knowledge that she had been unable to produce an heir to guarantee a Catholic succession and that her Protestant sister Elizabeth was to inherit the crown.

Below: 'Bloody Mary'. England's first reigning queen was a woman of strong convictions, iron will and ruthlessness.

CHAPTER TWO

THE AGE OF ELIZABETH

1558–1603

The 45–year reign of the last of the Tudors, Queen Elizabeth I, was a time of triumphant English achievement. The might of the Spanish Armada was repelled, adventurers such as Sir Walter Raleigh set foot fearlessly in the New World, naval heroes such as Sir Francis Drake proved England's daring and might on the high seas, and such geniuses as dramatist William Shakespeare, artist Nicholas Hilliard and composer William Byrd hit unprecedented artistic heights. In these proud years Elizabeth kept peace at home and established England as a major player on the world stage: her people recovered from the bloody religious conflict of the reigns of King Edward VI and Queen Mary and became confident in their own abilities, her country a vibrant success.

In these years, too, the English people came to love and revere their monarch as never before or, arguably, since – in the state-proclaimed mythology of the 'Virgin Queen', Elizabeth was married not to some foreign prince but to her own realm. In her final speech to Parliament, this great queen declared herself a happy instrument of God in serving and loving her people: 'For myself I was never so much enticed with the glorious name … or royal authority of a Queen as delighted that God hath made me his instrument to maintain his truth and glory and to defend his kingdom … There will never Queen sit in my seat with more zeal to my country, care to my subjects and that will sooner with willingness venture her life for your good and safety than myself.' And she declared in unforgettable terms: 'Though God has raised me high, yet this I count the glory of my crown, that I have reigned with your loves'.

Left: In the celebrated 'Armada Portrait', Elizabeth remains regally composed while English ships see off the Spanish invasion.

ELIZABETH I

1558–1603

When Elizabeth came to the throne in November 1558 the country was in crisis, virtually bankrupt and recently deprived of its last French possession in Calais. England was demoralized and conquest by a foreign power was all too likely: both France and Spain, whose king had been married to the last Queen Mary, eyed England greedily. As Elizabeth rode into London that autumn she was greeted by cheering crowds. After the bloody turmoil and ultimate failure of Queen Mary's reign, her people wanted and needed success for the flame-haired princess, whose colouring and regal manner may have reminded them comfortingly of her father, Henry VIII.

PRAGMATIC PROTESTANTISM

Religious passions were running high. In the eleven years before Princess Elizabeth's accession, England had been transformed into a militantly Protestant country by her brother Edward VI, then changed back to a staunchly Catholic

---

ELIZABETH I, QUEEN OF ENGLAND, 1558–1603

Birth: 7 Sept 1533, Greenwich Palace
Father: Henry VIII
Mother: Anne Boleyn
Accession: 17 Nov 1558
Coronation: 15 Jan 1559, Westminster Abbey
Succeeded by: James VI of Scots, James I of England
Greatest achievement: Defeat of the Spanish Armada, 1588
Feb 1559: House of Commons urges Queen to marry
April 1559: Acts of Supremacy and Uniformity establish Elizabeth as the supreme governor of the Church of England
23 April 1564: William Shakespeare born, Stratford upon Avon
1568: Mary, Queen of Scots imprisoned by Elizabeth
1569: Catholic uprising in northern England
Feb 1570: Elizabeth excommunicated by Pope Pius V

2 June 1572: The Duke of Norfolk executed for plot to depose Elizabeth
26 Sept 1580: Francis Drake completes circumnavigation of world
1584–9: Foundation of England's first overseas colony, 'Virginia'
1585: Sends English army to back Protestant revolts in the Netherlands
8 Feb 1587: Execution of Mary, Queen of Scots
1588: Defeats Spanish Armada
25 Feb 1601: Essex beheaded for treason
Death: 24 March 1603, Richmond Palace, Surrey

Below: Signature of a queen.

A PRINCESS LEARNED AND WITTY

As a child, Elizabeth was unusually serious, with the gravity of 40 when she was only six, according to one sycophantic account. She received an excellent education that made her fluent in Greek, Latin, French and Italian and instructed her in history, Protestant theology, moral philosophy and rhetoric. She had a shrewd mind – later, as queen, she would write her own speeches – and a capacity to inspire devotion.

In the 1550s, her Greek and Latin tutor, Roger Ascham, praised her strength of mind, her perseverance and her memory which, he said, 'Long keeps what it quickly picks up'. He was also captivated by her beautiful handwriting and her musical skills.

Above: Elizabeth's tutor Roger Ascham was a Cambridge fellow and humanist.

realm by her sister Mary. In punitive campaigns enforcing first one religious orthodoxy and then another, hundreds of English men and women had gone to their deaths as martyrs. One of Queen Elizabeth's great achievements in the early part of her reign was averting further major religious bloodshed.

Elizabeth herself was a Protestant, although a pragmatic rather than a radical or passionate one. In Mary's reign she had been willing, under pressure, to submit to Catholicism. Once she became queen, she reverted to the Protestantism espoused by her mother Anne Boleyn. At Elizabeth's magnificent coronation in Westminster Abbey on 15 January 1559, she pointedly refused to witness the Catholic ritual of Bishop Oglethorpe elevating the Host (communion bread).

Protestantism was officially reintroduced in England under the Acts of Supremacy and Uniformity of April 1559, which recognized the queen as supreme governor of the Church of England and brought Cranmer's 1552 Book of Common Prayer back into use.

The religious settlement was not harsh on Catholics. The wording of the Holy Communion sentences did not endorse transubstantiation (the Catholic doctrine that the bread turned into Christ's body), but at least was possibly compatible with the Catholic faith – communicants were encouraged to 'feed on [Christ] in thy heart by faith'. Elizabeth, who declared that she would not open windows into men's souls, was certainly not about to return to the bloody imposition of orthodoxy.

A HUSBAND FOR THE QUEEN

At her accession Elizabeth was aged 25, and the question of when and whom she would marry to provide an heir loomed large. Even as a princess, in her sister Mary's reign, Elizabeth had received many offers – including ones from Duke Emmanuel Philibert of Savoy and Prince Erik of Sweden, which were both declined. She was also

the recipient of flirtatious attention from Queen Mary's husband, King Philip of Spain, and after Elizabeth's accession Philip renewed his interest with indecent haste, making a formal offer of marriage on 10 January 1559, less than a month after Mary's burial. Elizabeth declined. The following month the House of Commons issued a 'loyal address' to the young queen, urging her to accept a husband in order to produce an heir to the throne. However, Elizabeth declared that she had no intention of marrying at present and reassured the Commons that if she changed her mind then she would choose a husband who was as committed as she to England's safety.

Left: The Pelican Portrait of Elizabeth I, c. 1574, by miniaturist Nicholas Hilliard.

Above: Contemporary accounts suggest that Elizabeth combined her mother's beauty and wit with her father's natural authority.

Meanwhile, court gossips noted that the queen was extremely close to the young and handsome Lord Robert Dudley, later the Earl of Leicester. This was not the first time that Elizabeth had been associated with handsome men at court; she was even reported to have been involved with Lord Thomas Seymour as a teenager.

While Elizabeth was celebrated as 'the Virgin Queen' she remained close to Dudley and later in her reign had similarly intense friendships with elegant noblemen including Sir Christopher Hatton, Robert Devereux, Earl of Essex, and Sir Walter Raleigh.

THE VIRGIN QUEEN
ELIZABETH AND MARRIAGE

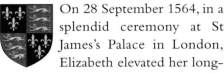

On 28 September 1564, in a splendid ceremony at St James's Palace in London, Elizabeth elevated her long-term favourite Robert Dudley to the earldom of Leicester, a position usually reserved for the king or queen's son, which brought many great territories with it. While Elizabeth officially remained the chaste 'Virgin Queen' and was the object of many a marriage proposal from European kings and princes, at court Dudley effectively lived as her consort, with apartments next to the queen in all her main places of residence and acting as her principal host at entertainments.

CULT OF THE VIRGIN QUEEN

Meanwhile, in 1563, after Elizabeth had suffered an attack of smallpox in December 1562, both Houses of Parliament petitioned her to take heed of the potential for a disastrous renewal of dynastic conflicts should she die unexpectedly and without an heir, and the House of Lords urged her to accept a royal husband.

This approach was the second time that the queen had been asked by Parliament to consider the succession, following an earlier 'loyal address' in 1559. In responding the first time, Elizabeth had declared, 'Nothing, no wordly thing under the sun, is so dear to me as the love and goodwill of my subjects', adding, 'in the end this shall be for me sufficient, that a marble stone shall declare that a queen, having reigned such a time, lived and died a virgin'. In her response in 1563, Elizabeth asked for MPs' trust and denied suggestions that she had taken vows of celibacy.

The cult of the Virgin Queen flourished: Elizabeth needed no princely husband, for she was married to her people. The language and behaviour of Arthurian chivalry and courtly love

informed life at court, apparently easing the confusion and difficulty caused by the role reversal of a woman lording over the country's most powerful men. The queen could use her 'prerogative' as a mistress to grant and then withdraw favours or defer decisions on difficult matters. The role suited a woman whose characteristic response to challenges was to be defensive and difficult to read.

Historians are divided as to whether Elizabeth's self-proclaimed virginity was a front or was genuine. Some have suggested that the queen was physically

Above: In 1560 Elizabeth rejected a marriage proposal from Erik of Sweden, acknowledging his 'zeal and love' but adding 'we have never yet conceived a feeling of that... affection towards anyone'.

incapable of having sexual relations; indeed, this was the report of her private physician, Dr Huick, in the 1560s. Others suggest that the queen would have been highly conscious of the potential political fallout should she become pregnant with an illegitimate child. To counter Dr Huick's evidence,

FAVOURITES OF THE VIRGIN QUEEN

Robert Dudley (1532/3–88) Handsome, ambitious and a long-term intimate of the queen, Robert Dudley was created Earl of Leicester and Baron Denbigh in 1564. Dudley recovered from Elizabeth's displeasure at his secret marriage to Lettice Knollys, the widowed Countess

of Essex, to become lieutenant-general of the army raised to counter the feared invasion of 1588.

Sir Christopher Hatton (1540–91) A beautiful dancer and accomplished in the traditions of 'courtly love', Hatton rose from the queen's bodyguard to become privy councillor and later Lord Chancellor 1587–91.

Robert Devereux (1567–1601) Cousin of the queen and her favourite towards the end of the reign, he inherited the earldom of Essex aged nine and was an experienced soldier. He had a fiery relationship with Elizabeth and often went against her wishes, yet retained her favour. However, in 1601 he tried to lead a revolt against her rule that led to his execution for treason.

Left: Sir Christopher Hatton became a royal bodyguard after giving up legal study.

Right: Robert Devereux often provoked the queen, but stayed in favour.

Sir Walter Raleigh (1554?–1618) Writer, soldier and adventurer, he delighted Elizabeth by asking permission to name territory he discovered in the New World after her: it was called 'Virginia' in honour of the Virgin Queen. He was knighted in 1585.

historians cite the reports of two medical committees at different times in the reign that certified Elizabeth to be capable of conceiving and giving birth.

A HATRED OF MARRIAGE

Elizabeth had a very strong dislike of marriage and was enraged when favourites or courtiers were wed. In the summer of 1579, when she found out that her great favourite of the early years, Leicester, had secretly wed Lettice Knollys, Countess of Essex, she claimed she would despatch Leicester to the Tower of London. In 1592 she found out that her later favourite, Sir Walter Raleigh, had not only married but also fathered a son, she went one better and actually jailed Raleigh and his wife

Right: Robert Dudley, earl of Leicester. Elizabeth once put down his attempt to insist upon a favour with the words 'I will have here but one mistress and no master'.

Elizabeth. The queen certainly had ample evidence to suggest that marriage was a risky and probably unrewarding enterprise. Her own mother's marriage had been brief and ended with the executioner's sword, and her sister Mary's marriage to Philip of Spain had

been a humiliating disaster. Marrying an Englishman would have encouraged factionalism by favouring one noble family above others. By refusing to marry, Elizabeth was able to retain full independence and avoid expectations that a wife – even a queen – should be obedient to her husband.

As Elizabeth aged, her virginity was presented and understood increasingly as self-sacrifice. Her image shifted from that of the virginal mistress to that of the virginal mother, with connotations of the Virgin Mary. Symbols such as the crescent moon and the pearl – once associated with the Virgin Mary – now became linked to Elizabeth.

Over the years, by staying clear of the international diplomatic unions into which so many of her regal predecessors had been drawn, she maintained the independent standing of her increasingly confident country, sacrificing her dynasty to maintain internal stability.

ELIZABETH AND MARY
COUSINS AND QUEENS

Queen Elizabeth's cousin Mary Stuart posed a potential threat to the English crown from the very start of the reign. Catholics considered the Protestant Elizabeth to be illegitimate, because they did not recognize Henry's divorce of Catherine of Aragon and marriage to Elizabeth's mother, Anne Boleyn, in 1533. The Catholic Mary Stuart – reigning as Mary, Queen of Scots since 1542 – had a viable claim to the English throne as granddaughter of Henry VIII's elder sister Margaret Tudor. Mary's was the second strongest claim after Elizabeth's, and she became a figurehead to Catholics for those wanting a return to the old religion.

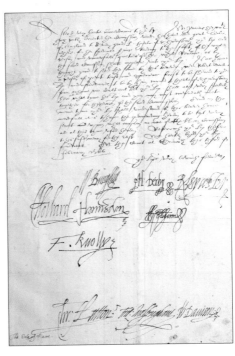

Above: In November 1586 MPs twice asked Elizabeth to order Mary's death. She signed the order on 1 February 1687.

COMPETING QUEENS

In England Elizabeth encountered no opposition to her claim as she was welcomed to London and crowned in Westminster Abbey on 15 January 1559. However, in France, Mary, Queen of Scots and her husband the Dauphin (heir to the French throne) began to quarter the English arms with the French arms in their emblem in a provocative gesture that could only be interpreted as a claim to the English throne either in the present or as Elizabeth's successor. It was a gesture that enraged Elizabeth.

Mary had acceded to the Scottish throne aged just seven days on the death of King James V in 1542, then been exiled to France for her own safety since 1548, early in the reign of Edward

Left: A French portrait of Mary Queen of Scots. Her execution ended plots to kill Elizabeth and replace her with a Catholic.

VI, while her French mother Mary of Guise (James V's widow) ruled as regent. In July 1559 Mary's husband Francis became King of France on the death of his father King Henry II, but after the former's sudden death aged just 16 in late 1560, negotiations began for Mary's return to claim her throne in Scotland.

The cousins were at loggerheads. Elizabeth initially refused to grant Mary safe passage to England; Mary would not recognize the Treaty of Edinburgh that accepted Elizabeth as Queen of England. Elizabeth would not name Mary as her heir.

Mary arrived in a Scotland that had embraced Protestantism and where government was in the hands of competing groups of fractious nobles. Over the ensuing eight years she tried and failed to win control. In a long and dramatic series of events she married her handsome Tudor cousin Henry Stuart, Earl of Darnley, gave birth to an heir, James, survived Darnley's murder and then unwillingly wed the probable murderer, James Hepburn, 4th Earl of Bothwell. In 1567 she abdicated under threat of death in favour of her one-year-old son, James VI. Then in May 1568, following civil war in Scotland, she fled to England for sanctuary.

LOYALTY TO MARY

Elizabeth refused to see Mary or to provide military or political support, but equally she resisted calls from Parliament and her senior advisors for Mary's execution. She would not consent to do away with Mary, even after a Catholic uprising in late 1569 in northern England. The rebellion was led by the earls of

Right: Mary's crucifix and rosary. During her incarceration, Mary had in her retinue a Catholic priest disguised as an almoner.

Northumberland and Westmorland in support of a plot to marry Mary to the powerful Duke of Norfolk and depose the queen. A royal army under the Earl of Sussex was victorious and the rebellion melted away, but Elizabeth exacted brutal revenge, ordering the hanging of as many as 900 rebels. She was merciful to Norfolk, who was spared the death penalty, placed in custody and released within six months.

Matters became more difficult still in February 1570, when Elizabeth was excommunicated by Pope Pius V, whose papal bull *Regnans in Excelsis* denounced the queen as a heretic and freed Catholics from their allegiance to her. After this, rebels could argue that it was the duty of devout Catholics to depose Elizabeth and replace her with Mary. In reponse, increasingly fierce anti-Catholic legislation was passed by Parliament. In 1571 Mary's position became more vulnerable again with the discovery of the 'Ridolfi plot', devised by a Florentine banker named Roberto di Ridolfi. It proposed that a rebellion led by the Duke of Norfolk, arranged to coincide with a

Above: Mary pronounced forgiveness on her executioners, declaring sadly 'I hope you will make an end of my troubles'.

Spanish invasion, would depose Elizabeth and crown Mary Queen of England. In the aftermath, Norfolk was found guilty of treason and executed.

AN END TO THE MATTER

Mary remained in captivity for 19 years and on 14 October 1586 she was found guilty of being involved in a plot to assassinate Elizabeth led by Derbyshire nobleman Anthony Babington. Elizabeth prevaricated for as long as she could, hard pressed by her councillors to condemn Mary, but desperate to find a different way of dealing with her cousin. She even tried to arrange Mary's assassination to avoid the need for an execution, but Mary was finally beheaded at Fotheringhay Castle in Northamptonshire on 8 February 1587.

Elizabeth appeared at once to regret what she had done, for she was maddened with grief at the news of the death, claimed she had not meant to send the death warrant and cast Sir William Davison, the secretary of state who supervised the warrant, into the Tower of London.

Mary's death may have caused Elizabeth private grief, but it was met by public rejoicing.

EUROPE IN THE TIME OF ELIZABETH
FRANCE, THE NETHERLANDS AND IRELAND

Elizabeth's foreign policy put defence first. Determined to avoid the large-scale foreign campaigns that devastated royal finances in the reign of Henry VIII, she preferred to use diplomacy and make low-key military interventions in furtherance of Protestant resistance to the might of Catholic France and Spain.

THE CATHOLIC THREAT

At the start of the reign, the main concern of the queen and her advisors was the threat of a Franco-Scottish Catholic alliance. The 16-year-old Mary, Queen of Scots was married to Francis, heir to the French throne; meanwhile, Mary's French mother, Mary of Guise,

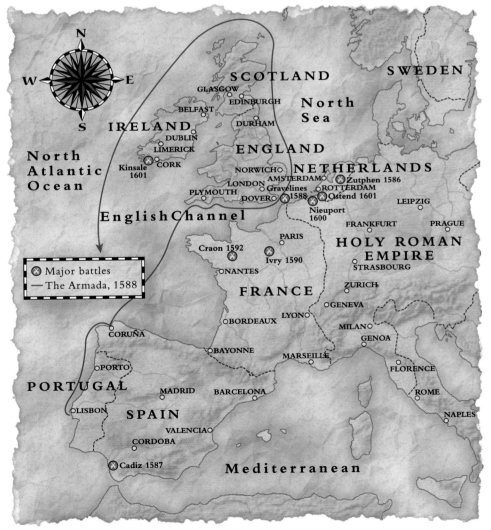

Above: The slaughter of Huguenots in the St Bartholomew's Day Massacre of 1572 horrified Protestants across Europe.

Left: Europe in the reign of Elizabeth. The most important military clash was the sea battle of Gravelines against the Armada.

ruled Scotland as regent. England was officially at peace with France, having signed the treaty of Cateau-Cambrésis in April 1559. In Scotland, Elizabeth provided aid to the Protestant Lords of the Congregation, who deposed Mary of Guise and attempted to drive out the French presence. Under the Treaty of Edinburgh in July 1560, a Protestant Regency Council was established. In France, too, Elizabeth supplied aid to Protestants seeking to undermine a Catholic ruler, and under the 1562 Treaty of Hampton Court she supported the French Huguenots.

AN ENEMY OF ROME

After Elizabeth's excommunication in 1570 and the discovery of the Ridolfi plot the following year, the queen came under pressure from her Privy Council

Above: Don John, Catholic scourge of the Dutch Protestants, wanted to invade England and marry Mary, Queen of Scots.

not only to execute Mary but also to take a more active role in Continental struggles between Protestants and Catholics. In 1572 the stakes were raised by a series of violent outbursts against French Huguenots (called the 'St Bartholomew's Day Massacre') that

resulted in the deaths of approximately 70,000–100,000 Protestants there. Queen Elizabeth quietly sent money and munitions to the Huguenots but publicly remained on friendly terms with the French Catholic regime.

DUTCH COURAGE

Elizabeth also backed Dutch Protestants in their rebellion against Spanish rule. In 1576 when Spain sent Austrian commander Don John to put down the revolt, Elizabeth was offered the sovereignty of the Netherlands if she would provide military force and agree an Anglo-Dutch alliance. She declined, but agreed loans and financial support totalling £120,000 to help the Protestant cause. She entered a formal alliance with the rebels in December 1577 but the following year the rebels were decisively defeated by Don John. In 1585, following the assassination of Dutch leader William of Orange and with war against Spain looming, Elizabeth agreed to send a 7,000-strong army to the Netherlands under the Earl of Leicester and to garrison the ports of

Above: The Earl of Essex. After failing to impose himself on Irish rebels, Essex was unable to regain the favour of the queen.

Flushing and Brill. Elizabeth's decision to help brought her the title 'Protector of the Netherlands'. In 1589, Elizabeth finally sent English troops into France, to back the claim of the prominent Huguenot, Henry of Navarre, to the French throne.

ELIZABETH AND IRELAND

Elizabeth's attempt to impose the Protestant religious 'settlement' of 1560 in overwhelmingly Catholic Ireland provoked a series of uprisings. The major disturbances were in the years 1569–73, 1579–83 and 1595–8.

June 1569: Military captain James Fitzmaurice Fitzgerald launches a Catholic revolt by attacking English colonists at Kerrycurihy, County Cork.

1570–2: Sir John Perrot, appointed to the new position of Lord President of Munster, wins the submission of James Fitzmaurice Fitzgerald and stamps out revolt in the province.

1579: Fitzgerald heads a new religious revolt, declaring Elizabeth a heretic, with secret support from both the pope and Philip II of Spain.

1580: English forces defeat the rebels. Lord Grey de Wilton, the queen's newly appointed deputy in Ireland, crushes an Irish garrison at Smerwick, Munster.

Nov 1583: Fitzgerald's cousin, the Earl of Desmond, is captured and killed by English forces under de Wilton.

1594: Hugh O'Neill, Earl of Tyrone, heads a new Catholic revolt, in Ulster.

May 1595: Sir John Norris is despatched to Ireland to put down the revolt, but fails.

14 Aug 1598: Tyrone wins a great victory at Yellow Ford, Ulster, over an English army led by Sir Henry Bagenal. The English commander and 830 English troops die.

April 1599: The Earl of Essex, the newly appointed Lord Lieutenant of Ireland, agrees a truce with Tyrone against Elizabeth's express instructions.

However, following accusations that Essex had made a treasonable pact with the Irish earl, he abandons his post and returns to England to explain his conduct to the Queen. He is later arrested, charged with maladministration and finally – on 25 February 1601 – beheaded for treason.

Sept 1601: The continuing Irish revolt is strengthened by the arrival of 3,400 Spanish troops.

24 Dec 1601: Charles Blount, Lord Mountjoy, defeats Irish rebels and their Spanish reinforcements in battle near Kinsale.

March 1603: Tyrone's revolt has not recovered from the 1601 defeat. He submits to Elizabeth and after her death receives a royal pardon from King James I.

THE ARMADA
A FAMOUS VICTORY, 1588

The defeat of the Spanish Armada in 1588 occupies a hallowed place in English history. Elizabeth's navy, commanded by Lord Howard of Effingham, forced the 130-galleon fleet of King Philip II of Spain to abandon plans for an invasion of England and to set sail for home. Around 15,000 Spaniards died in the encounter, compared with English losses of fewer than 100. Lord Howard afterwards declared: 'I do warrant you, all the world never saw such a force as theirs was'.

THE RUN-UP TO INVASION

The Armada invasion came after years of growing tension between England and Spain. King Philip, former husband of Elizabeth's sister Mary and a one-time suitor of Elizabeth herself, was increasingly enraged by Elizabeth's support for Protestant revolt against Spanish rule in the Netherlands and by the activities of English adventurers such as Francis Drake and John Hawkins in harrying Spanish colonial shipping.

AN INVINCIBLE FLEET

The impetus for Philip's military action was Elizabeth's 1585 despatch of an English army to the Netherlands and the 1587 execution of Mary, Queen of Scots. With the death of Mary, Philip saw that he himself could now lay claim to the English crown in the event of the restoration of Catholicism.

Philip had become king of Portugal in 1580 and so had access to the Atlantic port of Lisbon. The Spanish ships —

Above: Elizabeth gave the 'Armada Jewel' to Sir Thomas Heneage, Treasurer of War, to celebrate the triumph of 1588.

THE QUEEN'S SPEECH

In facing the threat of invasion Elizabeth was characteristically fearless, inspirational and defiant. On 9 August, before it was clear at home that the Armada was a spent force, she visited the troops assembled at Tilbury in Essex under the command of the Earl of Leicester. As her army prepared to repel a Spanish force commanded by the Duke of Parma, King Philip's regent in the Netherlands, Elizabeth rode among them, wearing a steel breastplate and seated on a grey gelding, to deliver a stirring speech that lived long in popular memory. Onlooker James Aske likened her to a 'sacred general'.

'My loving people, We have been persuaded by some that are careful of our safety to take heed how we commit ourselves to armed multitudes for fear of treachery, but I assure you I do not desire to live to distrust my faithful and loving people. Let tyrants fear…I have always so behaved myself that, under God, I have placed my chiefest strength and safeguard in the loyal hearts and good will of my subjects, and therefore I am come amongst you as you see at this time, not for my recreation and disport, but being resolved, in the midst and heat of the battle, to live or die amongst you all, to lay down for my God and for my kingdom, and for my people, my honour and my blood, even in the dust. I know I have the body of a weak and feeble woman, but I have the heart and stomach of a king, and of a king of England too, and think it foul scorn that Parma or Spain or any Prince of Europe should dare invade the borders of my realm, to which, rather than any dishonour shall grow by me, I myself will take up arms, I myself will be your general, judge and rewarder of every one of your virtues in the field. I know already for your forwardness you have deserved rewards and crowns; and we do assure you, on the word of a Prince, they shall be duly paid to you….By your valour in the field, we shall shortly have a famous victory over these enemies of my God, of my kingdom and of my people.'

Left: A painted 17th-century panel from St Faith's Church at Gaywood, Norfolk, shows Elizabeth arriving at Tilbury.

Above: Spanish ships flounder in the teeth of a south-west wind. This image of the sea battle off Gravelines is by Nicholas Hilliard.

ironically dubbed *El Armada Invencible* ('The Invincible Fleet') – set sail from there on 30 May 1588 under the command of the Duke of Medina Sidonia.

The plan was to sail to the Netherlands and ferry 16,000 Spanish troops from there to England, where they would support a popular uprising among Catholic sympathizers in the south-west. Philip's ultimate goal was to sweep Elizabeth from the throne and restore freedom of Catholic worship in England. He sent his admiral, the Duke of Medina Sidonia, on what he saw as a sacred mission, with these words ringing in his ears. 'If you fail, you fail; but the cause being the cause of God, you will not fail.'

SPANISH SEA POWER WRECKED

The fleet of some 130 ships had a troubled voyage northwards and was forced by storms into the northern Spanish port of Coruña; it did not reach the Channel for over two months. The English watched and waited and finally sighted the Armada off the Lizard coast of Cornwall on 29 July. As news of the invasion threat was spread across southern England by messengers and hilltop beacons, Francis Drake and Lord Howard put to sea with about 120 ships. They engaged the Spanish fleet three times – off Eddystone, off Portland and near the Isle of Wight – before the Armada anchored out from Calais, the former English possession in France.

Then in a dramatic midnight mission conceived by Lord Howard's vice-admiral, none other than Sir Francis Drake, empty English fireships stocked with wood and explosives were sent in and, helped by strong winds, created a wall of fire among the Spanish ships.

Below: Drake's drum. Over the years since 1588 its ghostly roll has reputedly been heard at times of English deliverance – such as the German navy's surrender in 1918.

The Spanish galleons put to sea in a panic and, in the face of storming southwest winds were unable to regroup before the English ships attacked again off Gravelines. The chief ships of the English fleet, the 20 royal galleons, were faster than the Spanish ships, more manoeuvrable, better armed and bigger.

With his fleet in disarray and having already lost 2,000 men in a week of fighting the superior English fleet, the Duke of Medina Sidonia ordered retreat. The wind forced the Armada to sail not back down the English Channel, but north up the east coast of England and Scotland, hoping to round the Orkneys and the Hebrides and regain the relative safety of the Atlantic Ocean. They were harried by English ships as far as Scottish waters and in the Atlantic were hit by storms. By the time that the fleet arrived back home it had lost at least 63 ships and around half of its 30,000 men.

The defeat was a key event of Elizabeth's reign. As well as safeguarding Elizabeth's religious settlement and preventing a potential bloodbath in England, it boosted the reputation of the English fleet and consolidated the growing self-confidence of the English. The victory also marked a shift in power from Catholic southern Europe to Protestant northern countries.

VOYAGES OF DISCOVERY
GLOBAL EXPLORATION

In the service of the great Queen Elizabeth, English adventurers such as Sir Francis Drake, Sir Martin Frobisher, Sir John Hawkins and Sir Walter Raleigh tamed the high seas as they made voyages of exploration, piracy and colonization around the globe.

LAND OF THE 'VIRGIN QUEEN'

Under Elizabeth, England founded its first short-lived overseas colony, named Virginia in honour of the Virgin Queen, at Roanoke Island, now North Carolina in the years 1584–9. Virginia was established by one of Elizabeth's principal favourites, Sir Walter Raleigh, who in the 1580s was employed at court and in trade in London; he did not visit the New World himself until later years. In 1584, however, he sent two men, Philip Amadas and Arthur Barlowe, to find a site for a colony, and upon their return with promising reports, he despatched 107 settlers under the command of Sir Richard Grenville in 1585. The first group, discouraged by

Below: Scourge of Spain. Sir Francis Drake was known as El Draque *('the Dragon') by his Spanish foes.*

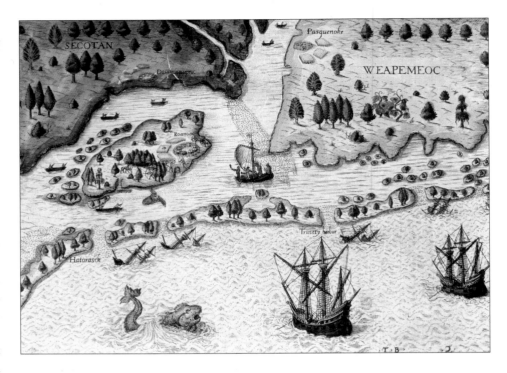

Native American attacks, abandoned the settlement and returned to England, but Raleigh sent a second group of around 150 settlers in 1587. The settlers built houses, but their commander, John White, sailed to England for further supplies and was delayed in returning because of the Spanish Armada's threat. When he did return in 1590 he found the colony had mysteriously vanished – the only clue was the word 'Croatoan' cut in a tree trunk. The attempt to establish the colony was abandoned.

Raleigh did later lead a New World voyage: in 1595 he explored what is now Venezuela and sailed the Orinoco river in search of the legendary city of gold, Manoa, which was said to be ruled by a king named 'El Dorado'.

SIR FRANCIS DRAKE

The most celebrated of Elizabeth's roving seafarers, Francis Drake, first made his name and fortune in a voyage to South America and Panama in 1572–3. He set sail from Plymouth on 24 May 1572, with a privateering commission from the queen; essentially the permis-

Above: This contemporary engraving of the arrival of the English in Virginia was made by Theodore de Bry (1528–98).

sion to plunder Spanish territories and riches. A militant Protestant, he saw it not only as profitable but as a religious duty to plunder Catholic Spain. In Panama he attacked the Spanish settlement of Nombre de Dios and left with great riches before exploring the Isthmus of Panama on foot and, from a tree on high ground, becoming the first Englishman to see the Pacific Ocean. He captured a Spanish caravan and took large amounts of silver to add to his plunder from attacking Spanish shipping on the high seas and returned to England with the most astonishing haul of New World riches yet seen.

Drake next departed in 1577 on a voyage to explore South America and the South Pacific, where a vast hidden continent was rumoured to exist. Before his departure he had an audience with Queen Elizabeth, who told him she hoped he could win some measure of revenge for various slights against her by

Above: England's first slave trader and a cousin of Sir Francis Drake, Sir John Hawkins explored Guinea and the Spanish West Indies.

Hind was weighed down with glittering treasures and exotic spices. On 4 April 1581, Queen Elizabeth — secretly delighted at the damage Drake had done to Spanish interests — came aboard the *Golden Hind* on the Thames at Deptford and knighted Sir Francis. The Spanish ambassador was outraged.

Sir Francis Drake was now a trusted royal servant. In 1587 Elizabeth sent him to attack Spain's empire: on this voyage he plundered Spanish settlements in the Cape Verde Islands, Colombia, Florida and Hispaniola (the Dominican Republic and Haiti).

FROBISHER AND HAWKINS

Another of Queen Elizabeth's free-ranging 'privateers' was Martin Frobisher, who led three voyages to Baffin Island and Labrador in search of gold mines in 1576–8, the second two with the queen's financial investment. He left his name in Frobisher Bay (south-eastern Baffin Island), but failed to find any gold. Like Raleigh, Frobisher also attempted to establish a New World colony, but failed. Subsequently, he sailed with Drake to the West Indies in 1585 and was knighted for his services to the queen in defeating the Armada.

Sir John Hawkins was England's first slave trader. After making a great fortune in a pioneering 1562–3 voyage financed by London merchants in which he sold Africans captured in Guinea as slaves in

Above: Sir Walter Raleigh was a natural philosopher as well as an adventurer. He was fascinated by potential uses of mathematics as a navigational aid.

the king of Spain. He set sail in the *Golden Hind* in December 1577. Reaching South America, he sailed through the Strait of Magellan and entered the Pacific, then sailed up the western coast of the continent, winning rich pickings from Spanish ships and colonial settlements, before trying and failing to find the Northwest Passage. Anchoring off the area of modern San Francisco, he claimed the land for Queen Elizabeth and dubbed it 'New Albion'. From there he sailed westwards across the Pacific, then home across the Indian Ocean and around the Cape of Good Hope to the Atlantic.

Drake landed at Plymouth on 26 September 1580 to complete his circumnavigation of the world; the first by an Englishman and only the second ever, following that by Portuguese captain Ferdinand Magellan. The *Golden*

the Spanish West Indies, he won the queen's backing for a second successful trip in 1564–65. A third trip with his relative, Francis Drake, nearly ended in disaster, however.

Later Hawkins was responsible for supervising the construction of the swift, well-armed ships that outgunned the galleons of the Spanish navy in 1588. He was knighted for his part in England's great victory.

Right: Exploration routes to the Americas and the Far East followed by some of Elizabeth's fearless naval pioneers.

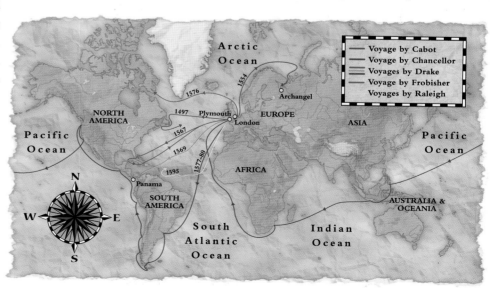

ELIZABETH'S COURT
A GLITTERING PRESENCE

In July 1575 the Earl of Leicester laid on lavish celebrations for Elizabeth and her travelling court at Kenilworth Castle, in Warwickshire, which had been a gift from the queen ten years earlier.

AN ARCADIAN FANTASY

At enormous expense, the castle and grounds were transformed into a chivalric and arcadian fantasy. Leicester gave over to Elizabeth an entire, extravagantly decorated wing of the building and flooded a field in front of the castle to make an artificial lake. As she arrived, Elizabeth was greeted by a boy dressed as a nymph on an island in the lake. He declaimed the words, 'The Lake, the Lodge, the Lord are yours for to command.' At the castle gates a scholar disguised as Hercules hailed the queen in blank verse. As she entered, the clocks were stopped – time would stand still while the queen was in residence.

The queen stayed at Kenilworth for 18 days of hunting, dancing, feasting and elaborate pageants. On one evening, a

Below: Elizabethan noblemen kept alive the traditions of knightly chivalry revived under Edward III and popular in the reign of Elizabeth's father, Henry VIII.

banquet of 300 dishes was provided, on another Elizabeth greatly enjoyed a play, *The Slaughter of the Danes at Hock Tide,* put on by the Men of Coventry.

At every turn, Leicester had laid on surprises and entertainments. When the queen complained that she could not view the castle gardens from the window of her bedchamber, Leicester secretly had a garden laid out in the

Above: The queen's glory. Admirers crowd close as Elizabeth, a shimmering white vision in a sedan chair, is carried past.

course of one night so that when she awoke, she might find that her wish had been granted.

The events at Kenilworth were part of Elizabeth's majestic 'summer progress' in 1575 when, with Leicester as her guide, she made a series of visits to country houses across central England. In these 'progresses', held each year, Elizabeth descended upon her nobles and people to impress all with her glittering magnificence. She travelled with some 300 wagons and 2,000 horses, either riding on horseback or carried in a litter. Country folk lined the roads to watch this vision of regal power pass.

COURTLY FASHIONS

By the 1570s, Elizabeth's court was a place of extravagant display, whose running costs had reached several hundred pounds a week. Elizabeth had a huge abundance of dresses, jewellery and precious stones, since she received vast numbers of jewels as gifts from ambassadors, courtiers and suitors. Each New Year's Day was a time of ceremonial gift-giving, when the Queen received dresses, jewellery, gloves, petticoats and other presents from leading courtiers. On New Year's Day 1588, Sir Christopher Hatton gave Elizabeth a gold necklace and earrings set with

NONSINE SOLE IRIS

ENGLAND'S GODDESS

From the 1570s onward, Elizabeth's accession day, 17 November, was celebrated as a national holiday, with bonfires, the ringing of church bells, services of thanksgiving and ceremonial tilts and pageants at Whitehall Palace. It was a day of English Protestant pride that put half-remembered Catholic saints' days deep in the shade. Henry Lee, the Queen's Champion in tilting, initiated and organized the celebrations at Whitehall Palace each year until he retired aged 57 in 1590.

Above: This delicate miniature portrait of the queen by the great Nicholas Hilliard is found within the 'Armada Jewel'.

rubies and diamonds; the queen's jewellery collection was thought to be the most valuable in Europe.

Elizabeth's devotion to glittering display was, in part, a political decision to project herself as magnificence personified; a goddess on earth.

In 1575, summer progress celebrations were held in Warwick, where a vast firework display over the River Avon was backed up with the booming of cannon from the Tower of London, transported from the capital at the expense of Lord Warwick, Master of the Ordinance. The queen's encounter with town people and officials in Warwick is revealing of both her magnificence in their eyes and of her easy manner.

Above: A celestial presence. This portrait, by Italian Taddeo Zuccari (d. 1566), is one of many from the reign showing the queen lavishly dressed and smothered in jewellery.

When the town recorder was overcome with nerves at speaking in front of her, she called him forth saying, 'Come hither, little Recorder. It was told me that you would be afraid to look upon me or to speak boldly, but you were not so afraid of me as I was of you and I now thank you for putting me in mind of my duty'. When the firework display started a fire that damaged a house, Elizabeth summoned the elderly couple who owned the dwelling and offered to right the damage.

GLORIANA
THE REALM OF THE FAERIE QUEEN

Towards the end of the reign, the poet Edmund Spenser dedicated his allegorical chivalric romance, *The Faerie Queene*, to Elizabeth, 'by the Grace of God Queen of England, France and Ireland and of Virginia, Defender of the Faith, &c'. In the work, published in 1590–6, the Queen of Faerie land, named Gloriana, represents glory both in the abstract and in the person of Elizabeth. As Spenser wrote, 'In that Faerie Queen I mean glory in my general intention, but in my particular I conceive the most excellent and glorious person of our sovereign the Queen'. The poet presented the first three manuscript books of the poem to the queen at court in 1589.

Elizabeth was an enthusiastic and discerning patron of the arts, which burst forth in an extraordinary flowering during her reign. In addition to Spenser,

Below: A Christian warrior slays a beast in an engraving from the 1590 edition of Edmund Spenser's The Faerie Queene.

whose epic is considered one of the finest poems in English, the period produced dramatists William Shakespeare, Christopher Marlowe and Ben Jonson; musicians Thomas Tallis and William Byrd; and the renowned miniaturist artist Nicholas Hilliard.

FLOWERING OF DRAMA

London's first theatre was founded in Holywell Street, Shoreditch, by actor James Burbage in December 1576. At Christmas 1582, five plays were put on at court for the entertainment of Elizabeth and her current suitor, the

Above: William Shakespeare at 34, in 1598. By this time the playwright's work was already a favourite of the queen's.

Duke of Alençon. In 1583 'the Queen's Men' were one of the companies of theatrical players formed in London. Some probably fanciful accounts of William Shakespeare's life claim that he first came to London having joined the Queen's Men as an actor in his native Stratford in 1587.

Shakespeare's plays were first performed in London in the early- to mid-1590s. His early works included the histories *Richard III* and the first part of *Henry VI*, comedies *The Taming of the Shrew* and *Two Gentlemen of Verona* and the tragedy *Romeo and Juliet*.

From 1594, he was one of the Lord Chamberlain's Men, based at the Globe Theatre in Bankside from 1598. Elizabeth so much enjoyed Shakespeare's *The History of Henry IV, with the Humorous Conceits of Sir John Falstaff* in 1597 that she asked for a new play showing Falstaff 'in love'; Shakespeare produced *The Merry Wives of Windsor*, which first played in 1600.

ELIZABETH'S PLAYWRIGHTS

Ben Jonson's dramatic genius is considered in some quarters to have been the equal of Shakespeare, but his major works were written after Elizabeth's death, when he was a favourite at the court of King James I.

The playwright Christopher Marlowe is believed also to have been an agent in Elizabeth's secret service, who was sent in 1587 to spy on Catholics in France. He also had a reputation as an atheist and blasphemer and, perhaps for this reason, the Privy Council issued an order for his arrest on

Qui voudra figurer, d'vn ouurage parfect,
La beauté, la Vertu, l'Ornement, et les graces,
De Nature, des Dieux, de l'vniuers, des Graces,
Accoure contempler la grand' ELIZABETH.

Above: This manuscript poem in praise of Elizabeth was presented to the queen in 1586 by its author Georges de la Motthe.

18 May 1593. He was killed in a tavern brawl in Deptford on 30 May 1593, probably over nothing more significant than the bill. His plays, which include *Tamburlaine the Great, The Tragical History of Doctor Faustus* and *The Jew of Malta*, were performed to great acclaim in London by the Admiral's Men and their star Edward Alleyn.

Nicholas Hilliard was the pre-eminent portrait artist of Elizabeth's day. He worked mainly in miniature – an art known to Elizabethans as 'limning' – and was also a jeweller and goldsmith. In 1572 he was appointed the queen's official limner. In 1584 he designed the queen's second great seal.

TALLIS AND BYRD

Queen Elizabeth recognized the musical genius of the great sacred composers Thomas Tallis (right, top) and William Byrd (right, bottom) by granting them a monopoly licence to print and sell music in England in 1575. In the same year, the two composers published *Cantiones Sacrae* ('Sacred Songs'), containing 16 motets by Tallis and 18 by Byrd. The book was dedicated to Queen Elizabeth. Tallis was by this time a man of 65 and had served as a gentleman of the Chapel Royal, the queen's musical body, since *c.*1542, well before the beginning of Elizabeth's reign. Byrd, Tallis's protégé, had joined the Chapel Royal from a position as organist at Lincoln Cathedral three years earlier.

THE REALITY BEHIND THE MASK
THE LAST DAYS OF ELIZABETH

Queen Elizabeth was very conscious of her public image. As early as 1563, the production of unauthorized portraits of the queen was banned. From the 1570s onwards, the projection of Elizabeth as the Virgin Queen, an earthly goddess or Protestant Madonna, was carefully managed. However, as she aged, the image of magnificence she wished to promote was increasingly at odds with physical reality.

THE EFFECTS OF AGE

Some authorities suggest that Elizabeth manufactured a glittering, magnificently costumed, jewel-laden public image to compensate for her waning physical charms. Essayist and philosopher Sir Francis Bacon, Lord Chancellor under King James I, wrote, 'She imagined that the people, who are much influenced by externals, would be diverted by the glitter of her jewels from noticing the decay of her personal attractions'. If this was a deliberate strategy, it largely succeeded, but it became more and

Below: William Cecil, Lord Burghley. Elizabeth was devoted to her great statesman, and in his final illness she sat by his bed and fed him with a spoon.

Above: Even the Faerie Queene was subject to the ravages of ageing. This portrait of Elizabeth in old age is by Dutch artist Marcus Gheeraerts the Younger.

more difficult to operate. The effects of ageing could not be avoided, even by the Queen, and beneath the laboriously constructed public face she became an old woman in a red wig, with bad teeth. In 1596, now aged over 60, she ordered the seizure of all paintings in which she looked ill, old or weak. In public, Elizabeth's age was clearly taking its toll: at the opening of the 1601 Parliament she found the velvet and ermine robes were too heavy and stumbled, falling into the arms of a peer alongside her. On a visit to Sir Robert Sidney around this time, she needed a walking stick to climb a staircase and appeared weary and forgetful.

CHANGE MUST COME

In the 1590s, Elizabeth was worn out and a little of the gloss had come off her reputation and achievements. Unemployment and taxation were both high, harvests failed in 1594–7, hard times led to rising crime rates and

TRUTHS IN THE MIRROR

For years Elizabeth avoided seeing herself in a looking glass, but in 1603 she commanded her courtiers to show her her true reflection, for the first time in two decades. She was devastated by the

sight of the sickly, 69-year-old face she saw in the mirror. By this time the ailing queen was close to death, stubbornly refusing food and medicine, resisting sleep, sitting forlornly on a floor cushion at Richmond Palace. She had been ill since late 1602. Her dearest friends and confidants were already dead: Leicester had died long before, in 1588; Sir Christopher Hatton, in 1591; William Cecil, Lord Burghley, in 1598; and she had sent Robert Devereux, Earl of Essex, to a traitor's death in 1601. Her favourite cousin, Kate Carey, Countess of Nottingham, died in late February 1603, and this was perhaps the final blow.

Left: A symbol of death hovers behind the now weary queen in this anonymous panel from Corsham Court, Wiltshire.

record numbers of executions for felons, Spain remained a threat and there was a troubling uncertainty over the succession. Some began to speak out against Elizabeth's rule, and to call for change.

Yet the mythology of the Virgin Queen was sustained to the end. Sir Robert Cecil laid on an entertainment for Elizabeth in December 1602, in which he celebrated her as Astraea, virgin of Roman poet Virgil's *Eclogues*: a just and saintly figure, whose presence on Earth brought a wonderful age of eternal spring and endless peace.

Elizabeth herself maintained her stance of devotion to her people: in her celebrated 'golden speech' to representatives of the 1601 Parliament she declared, 'I do not so much rejoice that God hath made me to be a Queen, as to be a Queen over so thankful a people', adding, 'I have cause to wish nothing more than to content the subject' and, 'It is my desire to live nor reign no longer than my life and reign shall be for your good.' As before, she used the language of love in place of a language of politics, casting herself as the mistress,

wife or mother of her country, driven always by care and devotion rather than duty or self-interest.

Elizabeth's own sun was preparing to set, but as the celebrated Virgin Queen she had no child to succeed to her throne. There were as many as a dozen people with at least a potentially viable claim to the English crown, including the Catholic Infanta Isabella Clara

Eugenia, daughter of Philip II of Spain and wife of the Governor of Flanders, Archduke Albert; Lord Beauchamp, a descendant of Lady Jane Grey's family; and the Protestant James Stuart, the son of her cousin Mary Queen of Scots, ruling as King James VI of Scots. Yet Elizabeth could not bring herself to name a successor, since this would involve accepting her own end.

THE SETTING OF THE SUN

Queen Elizabeth died at last in the early hours of 24 March 1603. According to some accounts she was unable to the last to name a successor, but did rouse herself on her deathbed to condemn the claim of Lord Beauchamp: 'I will have no rascal's son in my seat, but one worthy to be a king'. In other versions of events she was by now unable to speak and indicated by a movement of her hand that she wished the throne to pass to James Stuart. On her final evening she was visited by John Whitgift, Archbishop of Canterbury, who told the dying queen, 'Though she had been long a great queen here upon earth, yet shortly she was to yield an account of her stewardship to the King of Kings'.

Below: William Cecil's Burghley House. He entertained Elizabeth no fewer than 12 times at his various country houses.

CHAPTER THREE

THE UNION OF THE CROWNS AND CIVIL WAR

1603–1660

The royal House of Stewart – or Stuart as it came to be spelled in the late 16th century – had been ruling in Scotland for 232 years by the time King James VI of Scots travelled south from Edinburgh to take possession of the English crown as King James I of England in 1603. The first Stewart king was King Robert II (1371–90), who acceded as the son of Robert I the Bruce's daughter, Marjorie. Robert II's descendants ruled in a direct male line until the death of King James V (1513–42), when James's daughter Mary, Queen of Scots, began her troubled reign at the age of seven days. Mary's son, another James, acceded as James VI on his mother's abdication in July 1567.

On the Scots throne James proved himself an effective ruler, but in England his indulgence of favourites, authoritarian approach and apparent disdain for MPs provoked increasingly severe clashes with Parliament that worsened to the point of breaking during the reign of his son, Charles I. Charles had many opportunities to broker a mutually beneficial deal with Parliament, but his refusal to compromise was a key reason for the slide into civil war in the 1640s, which led to his conviction for treason and subsequent execution on a wooden platform outside the Banqueting House in Whitehall one freezing January day in 1649.

Left: This magnificent triple portrait of Charles I is by Sir Anthony van Dyck. As king Charles made a series of disastrous political decisions that hastened his own end and the monarchy's temporary abolition, but he proved a discerning patron in the visual arts.

JAMES I AND VI
1603–1625

 James VI of Scotland learned of his accession to the throne of England in Edinburgh on 26 March 1603, when a horseman brought news to Holyrood Palace of the death two days earlier of Queen Elizabeth I. After an emotional farewell to his own people, James began a prolonged procession through England, reaching London a month later, on 7 May. Everywhere, vast crowds were eager to see the Stuart king come to claim the throne vacated by the Tudors. James became James I when he and his wife Anne were crowned at Westminster Abbey on 25 July 1603.

THE KING'S DIGNITY

In person and manners King James presented a stark and unwelcome contrast to the regal dignity of his illustrious predecessor. A slovenly man, with over-prominent eyes, a large tongue that tended to make him drool and an unfortunate tendency to drunkenness and laziness, he could scarcely have made a greater contrast to the carefully stage-managed public persona of the Virgin Queen. Leading nobles – already somewhat suspicious of the elevation of a Scottish king to rule over England – resented James's expression of his homosexuality in infatuations with effeminate young men such as Robert Carr and George Villiers, both of whom he raised to high office. The king also had a forthright manner of speaking that was far removed from tact. It is said that when annoyed by the large crowds dogging his every move in London, he exclaimed 'God's wounds, I will pull down my breeches and they shall see my arse'.

Yet James's self-indulgent behaviour was allied to a vast intelligence and a highly educated mind convinced of the king's dignity and his absolute right to demand obedience. He had very diffi-

Above: Scots king on the English throne. James wanted to create, in his words, 'one kingdom…one uniformity of laws'.

cult relations with Parliament, which he treated with great tactlessness, often lecturing the Commons on their duty of obedience. Despite his appearance and behaviour, he saw himself as a man of regal bearing, dignity and authority.

'GREAT BRITAIN'

Early in his reign James attempted to combine England and Scotland in a unified kingdom of 'Great Britain'. This was the policy he presented to his first Parliament, called on 22 March 1604. The Commons was not convinced and resisted the union: one member complained that to combine the (Tudor) rose with the (Scottish) thistle might produce a monstrous result.

James defied them. On 20 October 1604 he proclaimed a new title for himself as 'King of Great Britain'. On 12 April 1606 a new Anglo-Scottish flag was introduced for shipping, combining

---

JAMES I AND VI, KING OF ENGLAND, SCOTLAND AND IRELAND, 1603–1625

Birth: 19 June 1566, Edinburgh Castle

Father: Henry Stewart, Lord Darnley

Mother: Mary, Queen of Scots

Accession: 24 July 1567 (Scotland); 24 March 1603 (England)

Inauguration/Coronation: 29 July 1567 (Stirling); 25 July 1603 (Westminster)

Queen: Anne of Denmark (m. 23 Nov 1589; d. 2 March 1619)

Succeeded by: His son Charles I

Greatest achievement: Peaceful union of the crowns of England and Scotland

1603: James recognizes Shakespeare's theatre company as 'King's Men'

18 Aug 1604: England is at peace with Spain

20 Oct 1604: James declares himself 'King of Great Britain'

Nov 1604: Shakespeare's great tragedy *Othello* plays at court

5 Nov 1605: Gunpowder Plot fails

13 May 1607: English settlers found 'Jamestown' in Virginia

1611: King James Authorized Version of the Bible is published

1616: Native American princess Pocahontas meets James at court

23 April 1616: William Shakespeare dies

16 Sept 1620: Pilgrim Fathers leave Plymouth aboard the *Mayflower*

26 Dec 1620: *Mayflower* pilgrims found settlement of New Plymouth

1624: Virginia becomes King's Royal Colony

Death: 27 March 1625, at Theobalds, Hertfordshire. Buried in Westminster Abbey

---

THE 'KING JAMES VERSION' OF THE BIBLE

A new English translation of the Holy Bible, 'authorized' by King James, was published in 1611. James had proposed a new easily comprehensible English-language version of the Bible in 1601, before his accession in London, when he was ruling as King James VI of Scots. In January 1604, the idea was brought forward again by Oxford University's John Reynolds at a conference on the church, which was held at Hampton Court under Archbishop of Canterbury John Whitgift. James personally approved 54 scholars to work on the translation, of whom 47 were finally involved, working for seven years with the original texts as well as existing English translations. For more than three centuries the work – known as the 'Authorised version' or the 'King James version' – was the standard Bible in English churches.

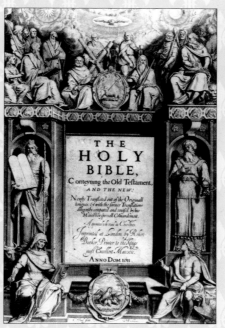

Above: The Authorised Bible, dedicated to James, 'principal mover and author'.

Above: Gunpowder, treason and plot. Victorian artist Sir John Gilbert represents Guy Fawkes kneeling before King James.

and restore Catholicism in England. It followed harsh new laws passed in 1604 against Catholics who refused to worship in Church of England services.

The plot centred on the opening of James's second session of Parliament, scheduled for 5 November 1605. Catholic lords led by Robert Catesby and Guy Fawkes planned to blow up the Palace of Westminster with gunpowder and then foment a Catholic rebellion in the Midlands. Details of the plan came out when one of the gang, Francis Tresham, warned his brother-in-law Lord Mounteagle, who would have been killed in the Lords by the explosion. Lord Mounteagle passed on the information to those in authority and the plot was foiled at the last moment.

the crosses of St George and St Andrew and called the 'Great Union' – or the 'Union Jack' (from 'Jacques', the French form of the king's name, which he preferred to use). Nevertheless, the instrument seeking to establish the union of the two countries was rejected in both Parliaments in 1607.

Another matter of pressing concern at the start of the reign was the need to bring an end to the ruinously expensive war with Spain. This was achieved with speed and efficiency – to a large extent, because Spain needed peace even more than England did – in a peace treaty signed in London on 18 August 1604.

THE GUNPOWDER PLOT

James's early reign was marked by rebellions against his rule. The first came in the very year of his accession, when Lord Cobham, Sir Walter Raleigh and other lords were arrested and found

Right: There was an outbreak of the plague at the time, but crowds still flocked to see the coronation of King James in 1603.

guilty of planning to depose James in favour of the king's cousin, Lady Arabella Stuart. On 10 December 1603 James spared Cobham at the very moment of execution, thus making a dramatic demonstration of his royal authority. The second and more serious plot aimed to depose the Protestant James

JAMES AND THE 'NEW WORLD'

THE SETTLEMENT OF AMERICA, 1603–1625

On 10 April 1606, James granted the Virginia companies in London and Bristol a royal charter to explore and settle land on part of the eastern seaboard of North America (roughly corresponding to the territory between northern Maine and Wilmington, North Carolina). Tudor adventurer Sir Walter Raleigh had founded the colony of Virginia, England's first in North America, but settlement there had foundered following the failure of the 'Lost Colony' of Roanoke.

THE JAMESTOWN SETTLEMENT

Three ships under the command of Captain Christopher Newport carrying 120 Virginia Company settlers set sail for North America in December 1606.

When they arrived in Virginia, in April 1607, they named the natural features of the area for the king and princes of the Stuart dynasty – the River James and Capes Henry and Charles – and honoured the king himself in the name of their settlement, Jamestown, which they established on 14 May 1607.

Under the terms of the charter, the land they claimed belonged to the king, with the settlers as sub-tenants of the Charter company. Jamestown had

the distinction of becoming the first permanent English settlement in North America. Government was undertaken by a royal council that was appointed by the king in London.

THE PRINCESS POCAHONTAS

Jamestown came under regular attack by local Native American Algonquians. One of the settlement leaders, Captain John Smith, was kidnapped and held by the Algonquian chief Wahunsonacock, or Powhatan, for four weeks, during which he survived a form of life or death trial in which, the story goes, his life was saved by Powhatan's 11-year-daughter, Pocahontas. Smith was released, became president of the Jamestown council and then was injured by a gunpowder burn and returned to England.

Pocahontas became a regular visitor to the Jamestown settlers, even bringing them gifts of food to help them survive. However, in 1613 one settler, Captain Samuel Argall, repaid her generosity by kidnapping her and holding her to ransom. He demanded the return of English prisoners and stolen firearms plus 'payment' of corn.

Pocahontas's father, Powhatan, paid a part of the ransom, but while Pocahontas was in captivity she was baptized a Christian as 'Lady Rebecca'

Above: This 1609 advertisement promises 'most Excellent fruites', but the first settlers of Virginia endured very lean times.

and fell in love with a European tobacco planter named John Rolfe. Pocahontas and John Rolfe were subsequently married and in 1616 sailed to England for a visit.

The Native American princess and convert was a great attraction in London society. Pocahontas was presented to King James I at court, and she sat with the king watching a masque written by the leading playwright Ben Jonson.

James was captivated by the young woman, and spoke of his plan to found a school in Virginia to educate young Native American children. Most unfortunately, before she and Rolfe could return to Virginia, Pocahontas contracted a fatal illness. She died in 1617 aged only 22.

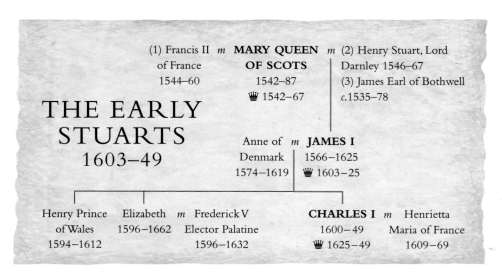

THE EARLY STUARTS 1603–49

(1) Francis II *m* **MARY QUEEN** *m* (2) Henry Stuart, Lord
of France **OF SCOTS** Darnley 1546–67
1544–60 1542–87 (3) James Earl of Bothwell
♛ 1542–67 *c*.1535–78

Anne of *m* **JAMES I**
Denmark 1566–1625
1574–1619 ♛ 1603–25

Henry Prince	Elizabeth *m* Frederick V	**CHARLES I** *m* Henrietta
of Wales	1596–1662 Elector Palatine	1600–49 Maria of France
1594–1612	1596–1632	♛ 1625–49 1609–69

THE KING'S ROYAL COLONY

A new royal charter of 1609 offered financial interests in the city of London the chance to invest in the Virginia colony. Government was in the hands of the Virginia company treasurer and his council in London, as well as that of a governor and advisory council in Jamestown. Profits were poor, because conditions were difficult and many ships were lost in the Atlantic.

Another royal charter, in 1612, widened the colony boundaries to include the Bermuda Islands and introduced a democratic assembly in Jamestown in 1619.

Conditions remained poor in the colony. James ordered an investigation: the result was that in 1624 he dissolved the London company and Virginia became the King's Royal Colony.

JAMES AND THE MAYFLOWER

On 16 September 1620 one of the most celebrated transatlantic voyages in history began under licence from King

Below: A map of Virginia, with scenes of its early settlement. The engraving was made and published by Thedore de Bry in the first part (1590) of a book on America.

James. Some 101 Puritans departed from Plymouth on board the *Mayflower* seeking a new life free from the religious persecution they suffered at home.

James and the Church of England authorities had been a major source of persecution for those – like many of the *Mayflower* pilgrims – who refused to accept the religious authority of king and church establishment. The king famously declared, 'I shall make them conform or I will harry them out of the land or else do worse'.

One group on board the *Mayflower* joined other travellers from the Netherlands: they were a congregation of English 'Separatists'. The 'Separatists' had been living in exile from James's persecution in the Low Countries for 12 years, since 1608. It was their declared belief that only Christ had authority over the Church.

Despite the fact that the *Mayflower* travellers had had major difficulties with the king, they sought and received royal backing for their venture before they departed. They won both the support of the Virginia Company and a licence from James after an interview in which the king was reportedly impressed by the adventurers' declaration that

Above: Pocahontas. This portrait is based on an engraving made during her 1616 visit to King James's court in London.

they would live by fishing. 'It is certainly an honest trade,' James responded, 'and was indeed the calling of the apostles themselves.'

Storms and high seas prevented the *Mayflower* from landing as intended in Virginia. The ship instead put in at Cape Cod (at the site of modern Provincetown, Massachusetts) on 21 November 1620 before unloading fully on 26 December at a nearby site that the new arrivals christened 'New Plymouth', 37 miles (60 km) south-east of Boston. William Brewster, leader of the Dutch 'Separatists', also became leader of the colony of New Plymouth. In 1621 the settlers in Plymouth gave thanks to God for the first good harvest of the colony with a three-day celebration to which they invited local Native Americans. This is celebrated in the modern 'Thanksgiving' holiday in the United States.

AT THE COURT OF KING JAMES
PLAYERS AND FAVOURITES, 1603–1625

The extraordinary 'English renaissance' of cultural life that began in the London of Queen Elizabeth continued in the reign of King James. In the first year of his reign James honoured William Shakespeare's theatrical company by making them the 'King's Men', and many of Shakespeare's greatest plays were performed at the royal court.

The tragedy *Hamlet*, first performed in 1601, just predated the new reign, but 1603 saw the first performance of *Othello* and the play is known to have been performed at James's court in November 1604. *All's Well that Ends Well* and *Measure for Measure* were first performed in 1604, *King Lear* in 1605, *Macbeth* in 1606 and *Antony and Cleopatra* and *Coriolanus* in 1607. The year 1611 was notable for the first productions of *Cymbeline*, *The Winter's*

Below: A scene from Ben Jonson's Masque of Queens *in the romantic style by Henry Fuseli (1741–1825).*

Tale and *The Tempest*. These later years also saw the publication of Shakespeare's extraordinary *Sonnets*, a collection of 154 poems printed in 1609 by the publisher Thomas Thorpe. The sonnets are mostly in praise of a young nobleman of great beauty, and the published edition was dedicated to 'Mr WH, the onlie begetter of these insuing sonnets'. Rival theories identify WH as William, Lord Herbert, or Henry Wriothesley, Earl of Southampton.

BEN JONSON AND THE MASQUE
In the years after 1605, King James, Queen Anne and their family and courtiers developed a great fondness for 'masques': theatrical performances with ornate costumes, choreographed dances and songs, often on classical themes. Rising playwright Ben Jonson forged a reputation as a creator of these entertainments. A clergyman's son and former bricklayer and soldier, Jonson had already made his mark in the late Elizabethan theatre world. His play

Above: 'Steenie'. This portrait of King James's great favourite George Villiers is by Flemish artist Paul van Somer (d. 1621).

Every Man in His Humour was performed at the Curtain Theatre in 1598 with Shakespeare himself in the cast.

Under King James, Jonson became a popular and well-rewarded figure at court. His first masque was created to give James's queen, Anne, the chance to make up and play a black woman: *The Masque of Blackness* was first put on to celebrate Twelfth Night in 1605. On the same day in 1610, Jonson's masque *Miles a Deo* ('Soldier of God') starred James's eldest son Henry in a performance to celebrate both the Christmas season and Henry's investiture that day as Prince of Wales. In these years Jonson also produced major plays, including *Volpone* (1605), *The Alchemist* (1610) and *Bartholomew Fair* (1614). In 1616 James granted Jonson a life pension: some scholars regard his court position as a forerunner of the 'poet laureate'.

In the first 12 years of the reign the poet John Donne (who was suffering from poverty after a secret 1601 marriage led to imprisonment and ruined his political prospects) made several

attempts to gain employment at court. He was repeatedly rebuffed by King James, who disliked his poetry and once declared, 'Dr. Donne's verses are like the peace of God; they pass all understanding'. James urged Donne to become an Anglican priest. When Donne finally agreed to enter the Church in 1615, James made him a royal chaplain and ordered Cambridge University to make the poet a Doctor of Divinity. Subsequently Donne won the favour of the new court favourite, George Villiers, Marquis of Buckingham, and with his support was made Dean of St Paul's, London. In addition to being a great poet, Donne was one of the greatest preachers of his day.

Also active at James's court was the architect and artist Inigo Jones, remembered as the founder of the English 'classical tradition' in architecture. Beginning in 1605, Jones made his name in London under the patronage of Queen Anne, designing the scenery and costumes for the court masques

Below: Shakespeare and friends. The great cultural figures of King James's London are portrayed by Victorian artist John Faed.

written by Ben Jonson. Then in 1615 he was appointed James's surveyor of building works. His first major work was the Queen's Palace at Greenwich, which he began in 1616 fresh from a 1613-14 tour of Italy in the company of Thomas Howard, second Earl of Arundel, during which Jones studied classical ruins and the work of modern Italian classical architect Andrea Palladio. Jones next rebuilt the Banqueting House in Whitehall in 1619–22.

COURT SCANDALS

King James's homosexual interest in and preferential treatment of handsome young men added spice to life at court. Early in the reign, the favourite was the 17-year-old Robert Carr (or Ker), the son of Scottish nobleman Sir Thomas Ker of Ferniehurst, who enjoyed a meteoric rise. The young man fell just as swiftly from favour, however, when he was found guilty of murder in 1616.

Around this time, James became enamoured of a new favourite, George Villiers, son of a Leicestershire squire. First introduced to the king at the age of 22 in August 1614, Villiers was made a gentleman of the bedchamber

Above: Shakespeare's fellow actors John Heming and Henry Condell prepared this first collected edition of his works (1623), known to scholars as the 'First Folio'.

in April 1615, Master of the Horse in January 1616, a Knight of the Garter in April 1616, Viscount Villiers and Baron Whaddon in August 1616, Earl of Buckingham in 1617, Marquis of Buckingham on 1 January 1618 and Duke of Buckingham in 1623. Villiers was tall and beautifully built with blue eyes and chestnut hair; courtiers reported that the king could scarcely keep his hands off the young man he called 'my Steenie', due to a supposed resemblance to St Stephen, who had 'the face of an angel'.

Buckingham made many enemies at court and among the aristocracy when he exploited his influence to raise his relatives to positions of power. He also succeeded in befriending the heir to the throne, Prince Charles, and travelled with Charles – in disguise – to Madrid on an unsuccessful attempt to negotiate a marriage with the Infanta, daughter of King Philip of Spain. Buckingham's almost entirely negative influence in government and at court lasted beyond the death of King James in 1625.

THE WISEST FOOL IN CHRISTENDOM
KING JAMES'S LEGACY, 1603–1625

James was dubbed 'the wisest fool in Christendom' by King Henry IV of France and he was certainly a king of contradictions: an intellectual who was a bawdy drunkard, a man who claimed regal dignity while behaving with none, a king who declared his divinely sanctioned authority but then allowed himself and his government to be dominated by incompetent 'favourites'. His reign was marked by repeated clashes with an increasingly troublesome and self-willed Parliament.

STRUGGLE WITH PARLIAMENT

As early as 1604 there were disagreements over the extent of the king's self-proclaimed royal prerogatives, and James's extravagance at court led to several angry encounters with Parliament over finance. When MPs refused to place a new series of import duties on merchants, James had the duties declared law by the courts in 1608 as he again

Below: King James left a difficult legacy for Charles I, particularly in the troubled relationship he had with MPs.

Above: The 'Plantation' of Protestants in 17th-century Ireland occurred mainly in the north, but also in pockets elsewhere.

Plantation and Settlement of English and Scottish 1556-1620

sought to undermine Parliament's role as supreme legislative body. This led Robert Cecil, Lord Salisbury, to propose a 'Great Contract' under which the king would abandon his royal prerogative to raise money in this way in return for a guaranteed annual grant of taxation. The contract could not be agreed, however, and in February 1611 James dissolved Parliament, angry at its failure to help him solve his financial problems.

The next Parliament of his reign was an unmitigated disaster. James called the Parliament in April 1614 on the advice of Sir Francis Bacon, the attorney general. James wanted the House to vote him money, but MPs were opposed to the king's foreign policy and refused to cooperate. The Parliament lasted only two months and did not pass a single piece of legislation.

James's third Parliament, in 1621, brought about a total breakdown of relations between king and MPs. This dramatic clash was largely fuelled by MPs' distaste for James's plan to forge an alliance with Catholic Spain and to negotiate a diplomatic marriage for his son Charles (the future Charles I) with the Infanta, daughter of the Spanish king. When Parliament demanded that Prince Charles seek a Protestant bride,

Above: England and Scotland. The Tudor arms were quartered with the lion rampant of Scotland in the king's great seal.

determined that the marriage should go through) made secret commitments to the French on improved conditions for Catholics in England.

A KING OF CONTRADICTIONS

By this time King James was unwell, severely troubled by arthritis and swiftly ageing. Government was almost entirely in the hands of his favourite, the Duke of Buckingham. James died on 27 March 1625 at his favourite residence, the country mansion of Theobalds in Hertfordshire, after suffering a stroke. He had been a king for all but one of his 59 years and, given the circumstances of his accession to the throne of Scotland in 1567, it was remarkable that he survived his youth to achieve such a long and largely peaceful reign.

A BLOODY INHERITANCE

James left a tragic legacy in Ireland. He backed the 'Plantation' or settlement of Catholic Ulster by Protestant Scots and Englishmen, which began in 1611. Ulster was one of the most strongly Catholic parts of Ireland and was actively rebellious against English government. Under the scheme, Catholic landowners' estates were confiscated and six new counties of Tyrone, Donegal, Armagh, Fermanagh, Derry and Cavan were created. The land was given to Protestant settlers. The 'Plantation', under plans enthusiastically approved by King James in 1608, added further fuel to flames of religious conflict in the region.

that James declare war on Spain and that existing anti-Catholic laws should be imposed with greater force, the king was furious, telling MPs that they had no right to meddle. When MPs then made a protestation of their ancient privileges and declared that every member should enjoy freedom of speech, James dissolved Parliament once more on 30 December 1621. He ripped from the House of Commons journal the pages on which the 'protestation' had been written.

A fourth Parliament, in March 1624, again urged war against Spain and an end to marriage negotiations with the Infanta. Later that year the proposed Spanish marriage – which had been very unlikely since the failure of a diplomatic trip to Spain by Charles and the Duke of Buckingham in 1623 – was replaced with a French match: in November 1624 Charles was betrothed to Henrietta Maria, the 15-year-old sister of King Louis XIII of France. During negotiations James (under pressure from Buckingham, who was

Right: James enjoyed hearing sermons. He patronized John Donne, whom he appointed Dean of St Paul's Cathedral in London.

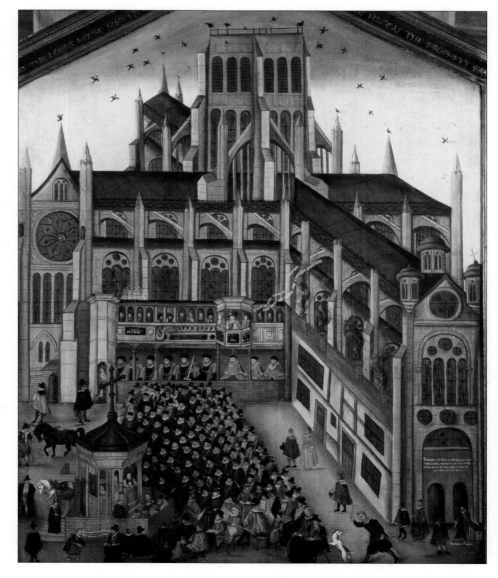

CHARLES I
1625–1649

Charles I's belief in his right to absolute and divinely sanctioned rule was allied to a haughty manner, a refusal to change his mind and a damaging willingness to do anything to have his way. These characteristics made him profoundly ill-suited for the task history set him, of handling a troublesome Parliament and maintaining peace between religious factions. His failure led to civil war, his own execution, the abolition of the monarchy and Britain's reinvention as a 'commonwealth'.

Born in Dunfermline Palace in 1600, Charles was six years the junior of Prince Henry, heir to the throne. Charles was a sickly child, so feeble that he did not walk until he turned seven in 1607, and at first he was left behind in Scotland when James progressed southwards to claim the throne of England. However, in 1612 he became heir to the throne, when Henry died of typhoid, and thereafter he grew in confidence. He had a lonely childhood, missing Henry and his sister Elizabeth, who left England in 1613 when she married Frederick, the Elector Palatine of the Rhine. As an adult Charles remained short – he grew no taller than 5ft 4in (1.6m) – and was frail and shy, with a minor speech defect that he never conquered.

Above: Charles I was 24 when he became king. He remained under the disastrous influence of the Duke of Buckingham.

INFLUENCE OF BUCKINGHAM

Life at Charles's court was rather more civilized than it had been under the often boorish King James I. Charles was a believer in the importance of manners, ritual and appearances, and he was a keen patron of the arts with a very fine eye for painting. However, in one important sense, government and court life were unchanged: George Villiers, the Duke of Buckingham was

a favourite of Charles, just as he had been of James, and he continued to exert a largely disastrous influence.

MPs were strongly critical of the Duke of Buckingham's disastrous diplomacy and military leadership. The duke's poorly resourced and incompetently led attack on Cadiz was driven back by Spain with humiliating ease in early summer 1626; in June 1626 Charles dissolved the second Parliament

Left: This medal was struck in 1633 to mark the king's return to London following his Scottish coronation in Edinburgh.

Left: A contemporary woodcut depicts Charles's visit to Spain, before he became king, to negotiate a planned marriage.

Buckingham's death at the hands of a knife-wielding assassin in 1628. The killer, who stabbed Buckingham at the *Greyhound Inn* in Portsmouth, as the duke prepared for yet another raid on La Rochelle, was found to be John Felton, a disgruntled veteran of the previous La Rochelle campaign. He made himself many new friends by despatching the enemy of the House of Commons.

RELIGIOUS TENSIONS HEAT UP

One of Charles's first acts as king was to welcome his new bride to England. In May 1625, Charles and the princess Henrietta Maria, daughter of France's King Henry IV and Queen Marie

of his reign after MPs called for the Duke of Buckingham's impeachment. Buckingham, in 1627, led one of two failed attacks to help the Huguenots who were besieged in the French port of La Rochelle; in June 1628 MPs called again for Buckingham to be dismissed from court and government. The sorry saga finally ended with

Above: Charles married Henrietta Maria in 1625. Their first son, Charles James, was born and died on 13 May 1629.

de'Medici, were married by proxy, and the following month Henrietta Maria landed at Dover from her homeland. Although the Catholic princess was not the Protestant bride that the English Commons and people had hoped for, she was generally preferred to James and Charles's original choice – the Catholic Infanta, daughter of the Spanish king.

Unfortunately, religious tension interfered with Charles's coronation in February 1626: Henrietta Maria refused to attend because the ceremony was performed by a Protestant bishop. She also grew angry over Charles's failure to honour promises made by his father James in the marriage agreement that conditions for English Catholics would be improved.

Religious differences also led to the dissolution of Charles's first Parliament, in August 1625: Charles took offence at MPs' repeated attacks on a clerical group known as the Arminians, who argued – with Charles's sympathy – for a revival of early Church doctrine. They were viewed by members of the 'reformed religion' as Catholics.

CHARLES I, KING OF ENGLAND, SCOTLAND AND IRELAND, 1625–1649

Birth: 19 Nov 1600, Dunfermline Palace

Father: James VI of Scots (later James I of 'Great Britain')

Mother: Anne of Denmark

Accession: 27 March 1625

Coronation: 2 Feb 1626, Westminster Abbey; 18 June 1633, Holyrood Palace, Edinburgh

Queen: Henrietta Maria (m. 13 June 1625; d. 21/31 August 1669)

Succeeded by: His son Charles II in Scotland; after Charles I was executed in 1649, the monarchy was abolished and England declared a commonwealth

Greatest achievement: Dignity with which he faced trial and execution

23 Aug 1628: Buckingham assassinated

10 March 1629: Dissolves Parliament and declares he will rule alone

April 1630: John Winthrop leads Puritans into exile in Massachussetts

1638–9: Defeated in the First Bishops' War in Scotland

1640: Defeated in the Second Bishops' War in Scotland

12 May 1641: Execution of Sir Thomas Wentworth, Earl of Strafford

22 Nov 1641: Parliament passes Grand Remonstrance against the king

3 Jan 1642: Charles fails to arrest leaders of parliamentary opposition

13 Sept 1642: Civil war: Charles raises royal standard

23 Oct 1642: First skirmish, Battle of Edghill

25 Sept 1643: Solemn League and Covenant allies English Puritans and Scots Presbyterians

2 July 1644: Major royalist defeat at Battle of Marston Moor

14 June 1645: Decisive Parliamentary victory in Battle of Naseby

Jan 1647: After fleeing to Scotland, Charles is handed into the care of Parliament

20–27 Jan 1649: On trial before High Court in London

Death: 30 Jan 1649, executed in Whitehall, buried in St George's Chapel, Windsor

---

COUNTDOWN TO CIVIL WAR
CHARLES I AND PARLIAMENT, 1625–1641

In the late 1620s Charles continued to be in direct conflict with Parliament over two main issues – revenue and religion.

Following great unrest provoked by his imposition of a 'forced loan' collected under threat of imprisonment, in 1628 Charles was forced to approve a 'petition of right' that guaranteed his subjects freedom from, among other things, arbitrary taxation. Henceforth, no man might be 'Compelled to make or yield any gift, loan, benevolence, tax or such like charge, without common consent by Act of Parliament'.

The same year William Laud, a supporter of the controversial Arminian doctrine became Bishop of London.

In a dramatic development on 2 March 1629, MPs outmanoeuvred the king to pass laws condemning attempts to raise taxes without parliamentary backing and attacking efforts to impose Arminianism. Charles had instructed the Speaker of the House, Sir John Finch, to rise when MPs began to debate and so prevent any laws being passed, but two MPs – Denzil Holles and Benjamin Valentine – forcibly held the Speaker in the chair, while others locked the door against the king's messenger, Black Rod, who had been sent to dissolve Parliament. In this way they were able to pass the laws that Charles opposed.

As a result on 10 March 1629 Charles dissolved Parliament, announcing that he would rule without its backing.

Above: Charles I. Anthony van Dyck, court painter from 1632, is celebrated for his sensitivity to the character of his subjects.

Speaking of the Commons, he declared, 'I know there are many there as dutiful subjects as any in the world; it being but some few Vipers amongst them that did cast this Mist of Undutifulness over most of their Eyes'.

DEFICIT IN ROYAL FINANCES

Thereafter, unable to levy taxation with parliamentary backing, Charles had to come up with ingenious schemes of doubtful legality to raise money in order to cover a deficit in the royal finances that was running at £20,000 a year by the mid-1630s. The 'ship tax' was levied on coastal areas – officially to fund the Royal Navy – and afterwards extended to inland areas also. Charles also raised customs duties and revived venerable 'forest laws'. These allowed fines to be imposed on those who encroached on ancient royal forests and were now applied to areas such as Essex, which had been forest in the past but had since been cleared. Having bypassed Parliament, the king was acting with no apparent restraint – a landowner named

RELIGIOUS EXILES

In 1630 John Winthrop led a mass exodus of Puritans to the New World, in flight from what they saw as excessive Catholic influence at court. In 1629 they obtained a charter from King Charles to establish the Massachussetts Bay Company. The king understood it to be a commercial venture, but Winthrop and friends were determined to found a Puritan colony. Winthrop was elected governor of the new colony before departure. He set sail aboard the *Arbella* at the head of a fleet of 11 ships containing 700 people in April 1630. In America, he was re-elected a number of times as governor of the fledgling colony. He wrote a celebrated sermon, 'The City on a Hill', which cast Puritan exiles as parties to a special agreement with God to found a sacred society. Another quite different religious exile founded

Maryland, named in honour of Charles's queen, Henrietta Maria. Cecilius Calvert, second Baron Baltimore, was a Roman Catholic who received a grant of territory from Charles to establish Maryland in 1632. Baltimore founded the colony both as a commercial enterprise and as a place of refuge where Catholics could live and worship in freedom.

Right: George, father of Cecilius Calvert. The colony of Maryland was his idea, but he died before it was realized.

John Bankes challenged the legality of the extension of the ship money but lost his case in court, in June 1638, in a decision that served to increase bad feeling against the king.

The fear of Catholic influence at home was heightened by Charles's reissue in 1633 of King James's *Book of Sports*. This specified the sports that were permissible on the Sabbath – and offended Puritans who argued that the Sabbath should be kept free of all sports and recreations, including music. Worse still in Puritan eyes was the 1634 visit to Queen Henrietta Maria of papal legate Gregorio Panzani and the public knowledge that the Catholic Mass was celebrated every day for the queen in the palace in Whitehall.

LAVISH ARTS SPENDING

Meanwhile at court, despite financial troubles and increasing public ill-feeling at Charles's unusual means of raising money from his people, the king spent lavishly on the arts. He hired the finest artists and put together a collection of Europe's greatest paintings. He commissioned works by leading artists such as Peter Paul Rubens and Anthony van Dyck and in 1632 made van Dyck court painter. He hired Rubens to paint scenes of King James I's apotheosis on the ceiling of the Inigo Jones's Banqueting House in Whitehall. In

1634 van Dyck painted a celebrated equestrian portrait of King Charles and in 1637 the well-known *Charles I in Three Positions*.

The king bought works by Titian, Raphael and Mantegna for the royal art collection. He viewed the collection as an expression of his regal authority and dignity and wanted it to be the equal to that of any European royal house. To this end, he put the collection under the control of Dutch art expert Abraham van der Doort.

Left: John Winthrop, first governor of Massachussetts, believed that God had chosen him for sainthood in his lifetime.

Above: Van Dyck painted several imposing portraits of Charles, seeking to express the king's belief in his divine right to rule.

As in his father James's reign, masques were a popular form of entertainment at court, with many designed by the great Inigo Jones. Doubtless Charles enjoyed escaping from the troubling political and religious struggles of his day into a well-ordered world that honoured ruler and courtiers. Inigo Jones and Ben Jonson collaborated on more than 30 masques, but had a disagreement in 1631 after which other playwrights and poets including James Shirley and Thomas Carew authored the masques.

THE ENGLISH CIVIL WAR
1642–1649

The beginning of the long struggle that became the English Civil War can be traced to Charles's 1637 decision to impose on the Scots a Book of Common Prayer almost exactly the same as the one used in England. This provoked strong opposition among Scottish Presbyterians, who saw the move as an Anglo-Catholic assault on the purity of their religion: in 1638 they signed a National Covenant to uphold their faith. Charles first attempted negotiation, at a general assembly of the Church of Scotland, in Glasgow, in November 1638, and when that failed, he found himself faced by a Scottish Covenanter army. He raised a royalist force and marched north, but in the First Bishops' War could not defeat the Covenanters and was forced to agree peace in June 1639.

THE LONG PARLIAMENT
In April 1640, Charles called his first Parliament for 11 years to try to raise money for further military action in Scotland. He encountered concerted opposition in the Commons and so

dismissed the Short Parliament after just three weeks. He then went ahead with the planned campaign in Scotland, but the Second Bishops' War ended in another defeat and Charles was forced into both a humiliating peace at Ripon and into recalling Parliament.

This Parliament would sit until 1660 and is known as the Long Parliament. The king's opponents in the Commons

Above: Key figures of the Civil War, including the Earl of Essex (top left) and Cromwell (bottom, second from left).

had Charles's most able minister, Thomas Wentworth, Earl of Strafford, impeached and then executed under a bill of attainder in May 1641. Charles was forced to concede that 'ship money' and his other financial levies were illegal and that Parliament could not be dissolved without its own agreement. On 22 November 1641 the Commons then passed a 'Grand Remonstrance' listing Charles's many failings since his accession. It called for royal ministers to be approved by Parliament and for the appointment of a Parliament-nominated assembly to oversee church reform.

A Catholic uprising in Ireland led Charles to raise another army, and MPs, fearful that he would use it against them, demanded that he relinquish control of the troops. He angrily refused and, in January 1642, took the bold step

Left: Captive king. This woodcut shows Charles under house arrest at Carisbrooke Castle, Isle of Wight, in late 1647.

of entering the Commons with an armed guard to arrest ringleader MPs for treason. He came too late. The MPs in question had been tipped off and escaped into hiding on a river barge.

Charles now fled London, heading for northern England. Queen Henrietta Maria and Princess Mary left the country to raise financial support for the king in Continental Europe, and England prepared for civil war.

FIRST SKIRMISHES

Charles raised the royal standard at Nottingham on 13 September 1642 and began to move on London as the Parliamentarians gathered an untrained army under the Earl of Essex. The first major clash, at Edghill near Banbury on 23 October 1642, was a victory for the king, although the Parliamentarian army retreated in good order. A second clash at Brentford, west of London, on 11 November was also a royalist victory, but a third, at nearby Turnham Green two days later, saw the 12,000-odd royalist troops defeated by a 25,000-strong Parliamentarian force.

The royalist advance on London was thus turned back, ending Charles's chances of securing a quick victory.

HONOURS EVEN

In 1643 fortunes swung to and fro, with royalist victories in Yorkshire and the south-west followed by a Parliamentarian fight-back that again blocked the king's approach to London. A key event was the signing of the 'Solemn League and Covenant', which pledged alliance between English Puritans and Scottish Presbyterians and provided a Scottish army to support the Parliamentary cause.

The Scottish Covenanters provided crucial support to the Parliamentarian army at the Battle of Marston Moor on 2 July 1644, when the royalists were swept away by a crack cavalry force led by Oliver Cromwell. However, later in the year Charles defeated the Earl of Essex at Lostwithiel, in Cornwall.

THE TIDE TURNS

1645 was the decisive year. Although royalist troops in Scotland under Montrose won a famous victory over Covenanters at Inverlochy in February, in England the Parliamentarians established the highly disciplined 'New Model Army' under the command of Fairfax and Cromwell and won a series of important victories; not least the overwhelming defeat of Charles's army at Naseby, Northants, on 14 June. In November Charles retreated to Oxford.

In spring 1646, as the Parliamentarians prepared to besiege Oxford, the king fled in disguise. He escaped to Scotland, but was handed back to the care of the English Parliament in January 1647. Kept at first under house arrest in Northants, Charles was taken into army custody in June 1647 as a new civil conflict developed between the New

Above: Major battles of the English Civil Wars. Parliamentarians won key victories at Marston Moor and Naseby in 1644–5.

Model Army and Parliament. After a final victory over Scottish royalists at Preston in August 1648, the army took control.

On 20 November, General Henry Ireton presented Parliament with the 'Remonstrance of the Army', which demanded that Charles be put on trial for treason. Parliament still hoped to reach a compromise with the king and rejected the document.

On 6 December Colonel Thomas Pride reduced the Commons to a 'rump' that would be obedient to the will of the military. At Christmas 1648 Charles was brought to Windsor Castle. The army hierarchy was determined to achieve its aims: the trial and execution of the king and the abolition of the monarchy.

THE EXECUTION OF CHARLES I

1649

King Charles appeared on trial before a specially created 'high court of justice', consisting of 159 commissioners appointed by the 'Rump' Parliament, in the Painted Chamber at the Palace of Westminster on 20 January 1649. Security was tight: soldiers watched the movements of the crowd, guards perched on the palace roof and the high court president, John Bradshaw, wore a steel-lined hat to protect him from assassins' bullets.

CHARGED WITH TREASON

The king was charged with having governed according to his will and not by law, with having waged war 'against the present Parliament and the people there represented' and with having committed treason against his own people – a neat reversal of the usual definition of treason. Charles refused to defend himself, or enter a plea in response to the

Below: Charles tried to project an aura of authority despite losing control of his destiny. This portrait by Edward Bower (fl 1635–67) shows the king at trial.

charge, as he denied that the court had any authority over him. He declared, 'I would know by what power I am called hither…by what authority' and warned the court, 'Remember I am your king, your lawful king', adding, 'I have a trust committed to me by God, by old and lawful descent, [and] I will not betray it, to answer a new unlawful authority'.

'TYRANT AND PUBLIC ENEMY'

The trial lasted eight days. Witnesses described the king's physical involvement in the battles of the civil war, while alleging that he approved atrocities against the people and that he tried his utmost while in captivity to stir up and prolong the wars.

Sentence was passed on 27 January. The high court found the king guilty as a 'Tyrant, traitor, murderer and public enemy to the Commonwealth of England' and sentenced him to be 'Put to death by the severing of his head from his body'.

John Bradshaw, president of the court, addressed Charles for 40 minutes, declaring that when a king entered battle against his own people he lost his claim to their allegiance, and arguing that even a monarch was subject to the law as it issued from Parliament. Charles was shocked and upset to discover that

Above: Signatories of Charles's death warrant included army men Oliver Cromwell and Henry Ireton but not Sir Thomas Fairfax, army commander.

he was not allowed to reply. Instead, with the death sentence ringing in his ears, he was taken to St James's Palace to await his end. Just 59 commissioners of the 159 appointed signed the king's death warrant.

Below: The king faces his accusers in the High Court of Justice on 27 January.

'MARTYR OF THE PEOPLE'

The execution was planned for early in the morning of the following day, 30 January 1649. It was a bitterly cold day: Charles wore two shirts from fear that he would be cold and shiver, giving onlookers the impression that he was trembling with fear. He gave instructions for sharing out his intimate possessions among his children, including his gold watch and his Bible, and he received Holy Communion.

However, the execution was delayed because Cromwell was told that under current law a king's successor must be declared at the moment of a royal death. The king was forced to wait while Parliament drafted and hurried through three readings of a bill declaring it illegal to make a proclamation of succession. It was not until 2 p.m. that Charles came out from the Banqueting House in Whitehall on to the platform specially raised against its side, where a large crowd had gathered.

Charles walked forth confident and fearless and made a final statement, declaring his loyalty to the Church of England and arguing that the people should have no part in government, saying, 'A subject and a sovereign are clean

THE CULT OF THE KING

Mindful that Charles could indeed become a martyr in death, the authorities arranged for his burial in St George's Chapel, Windsor Castle, well away from the London crowds, rather than in Westminster Abbey. His embalmed body – with the head sewn back in place – was moved to Windsor by water and he was buried in the castle on 8 February 1649. The authorities outlawed public mourning and declared that there would be no state funeral for the king.

But they were unable to stop the tide of emotion that made a bestseller of a book of the king's supposed meditations and prayers in his final days. The book – *Eikon Basilike, the Pourtraiture of His Sacred Majestie in his Solitude and Sufferings*, ghostwritten by John Gauden, chaplain to the earl of Warwick – went through 40 English-language editions in 1649 alone, and was translated into many languages including French, Latin, Dutch and Danish.

Subsequently, with the Restoration of the monarchy, the 'cult' of King Charles I was encouraged and in 1660 Parliament declared the king to be a martyr and made him a saint of the Anglican Church.

different things'. He then proclaimed, 'I am the martyr of the people' and forgave those who were responsible for his death. His last words were, 'I go from a corruptible to an incorruptible crown, where no disturbance can be'.

Because the executioner's block was very low, Charles had to lie down rather than kneel. When he was ready he made a pre-arranged signal with his hands and his head was cut off with one blow. The assistant to the executioner held the decapitated head aloft and a moan – perhaps of grief, perhaps of horror at the killing of a king – was heard from the watching crowd.

Pandemonium broke out among the crowd as hundreds of people struggled to dip scraps of cloth in the royal blood.

Below: Charles was defiant unto death. Dutch artist Weesop painted this 'Eyewitness Representation of the Execution of King Charles I'.

COMMONWEALTH AND PROTECTORATE
1649–1660

On 17 March 1649 the MPs in the 'Rump Parliament' finished the job begun with King Charles I's execution when they passed an act abolishing the monarchy and making England a 'Commonwealth and free state'. The act also abolished the House of Lords and proclaimed Parliament 'supreme authority of this nation'.

There was still powerful opposition to be faced, however. In September 1649, Cromwell was despatched to Ireland to put down a royalist uprising among Irish royalists. He won devastating victories at Wexford and Drogheda. Then in June 1650, having been made Commander-in-Chief of the Commonwealth forces, Cromwell marched north to Scotland, where the Covenanters were promoting the cause of Charles I's son, Charles.

Cromwell won a resounding victory over a Covenanter army at Dunbar on 3 September 1650, but royalist opposition

Below: Army commander, England's Protector. True to his convictions, Cromwell twice turned down the offer of the throne.

Above: Cromwell's crown. This gold five-shilling coin was minted in London in 1658.

persisted, and on 1 January 1651 Charles Stuart was crowned King Charles II of England, Scotland, Ireland and France (the last title traditional), at Scone in Scotland.

In August that year Charles led an army of Scots and royalist sympathisers across the border and marched on London. However, Cromwell inflicted a devastating defeat on him at Worcester on 3 September, forcing him to flee in disguise and go into hiding.

GOVERNING WITHOUT A KING

Although Oliver Cromwell had made the Commonwealth safe, the execution of the king had created a power vacuum and the search for a stable form of government proved a difficult one. As Commander-in-Chief of the army, Cromwell was the dominant figure. He eventually became frustrated at delays in the Rump Parliament, which was supposed to be planning for the election of a new assembly.

On 20 April 1653 Cromwell declared the Rump Parliament dissolved, angrily telling the House, 'You have sat here too long for the good you do. In the name of God, go!' He did not act in order to bolster his own position, but his behaviour was painfully reminiscent of

---

A SUCCESSION OF PARLIAMENTS

13 April–6 May 1640: 'Short Parliament' dissolved by King Charles I after three weeks

3 Nov 1640: Charles I calls 'Long Parliament'; not formally dissolved until 16 March 1660

7 Dec 1648: Col Thomas Pride 'purges' the Long Parliament to create the compliant 'Rump Parliament'

20 April 1653: Cromwell dissolves the Rump Parliament;

4 July 1653: New 'Barebones Parliament' assembles

12 Dec 1653: Barebones Parliament dissolved; Cromwell becomes Lord Protector

16 May 1659: Army leaders recall the Rump Parliament

Feb 1660: Members excluded in Pride's Purge are recalled to reconstitute the Long Parliament

16 March 1660: The Long Parliament votes to dissolve ahead of new elections

25 April 1660: The Pro-Royalist 'Convention Parliament' meets

---

the acts of Stuart 'tyranny' that had provoked the Civil War and led to the execution of a king.

KING OR LORD PROTECTOR?

A new Parliament was appointed, made up of 140 officially approved Puritans. The first parliament to represent the whole of the British Isles, it was nick-named the 'Barebones Parliament' from the name of one of its members, the Anabaptist Praisegod Barebones. It was short-lived, for in December 1653 it voted itself out of existence and put power into the hands of Cromwell. He thus became the first man to rule a unitary state of Great Britain and Ireland.

Above: 'In the name of God, go!' Like the Stuart kings before him, Cromwell dismissed troublesome MPs – including members of the Rump Parliament in 1653.

Major-General John Lambert was behind this development – essentially a coup – and he tried to persuade Cromwell to become king. Cromwell refused, however, providing proof of his religious sincerity and rectitude of character: he was convinced that it had been God's will for the monarchy to be abolished and he would not countenance its reintroduction. Instead he agreed to become 'Lord Protector'.

This change was introduced under England's first written constitution, the 'Instrument of Government', which made the country a Protectorate. Government was to be by the Lord Protector through a council of state and the House of Commons. Religious toleration was to be guaranteed for all, except Catholics.

When the new Parliament met in 1654 its attempts to alter the constitution and notably to restrict religious toleration led Cromwell to dissolve it once more. In July 1655 he introduced a new system of government under which 12 major-generals were appointed, with each ruling one of 12 English regions.

However, this system also proved unpopular and ineffective. Another House of Commons was elected in 1656.

In April–May 1657, the Commons again urged Cromwell to take the crown and become King Oliver, but after agonizing over the decision and, according to some accounts coming very close to accepting, Cromwell refused again. He declared, 'I would not seek to set up that that providence hath destroyed and laid in the dust'.

On 3 September 1658, Cromwell died aged 59. The extent to which he had become king in all but name, and in contradiction of his dearly held beliefs, was marked by the fact that he named his son, Richard, to be Lord Protector in his stead.

THE RETURN TO MONARCHY

Richard Cromwell's rule lasted only eight months. He resigned as Lord Protector when army leaders recalled the 'Rump Parliament' of 1648. The Rump Parliament could not impose its authority, however, and MPs and army still fought for supremacy.

In early 1660 General Monck, commander of the army in Scotland, marched to London and won the agreement of the Rump assembly to dissolve itself and recall the Long Parliament originally formed in 1640. This opened the way for a new election and another new Parliament and the prospect of a return of the monarchy.

A KING ON THE RUN

After the destruction of his hopes of regaining the crown at the Battle of Worcester on 3 September 1651, Charles II fled the battlefield in a charge of cavalry down Worcester High Street. He was on the run.

Changing into some old clothes and applying blacking to his face as disguise, he cut across country towards the sea. He attempted to take the ferry over the river Severn but, finding it guarded, he turned back to seek cover in woodland. By good fortune he met a Catholic royalist, William Carlis, who warned him that Cromwell's men were searching the woods. The pair decided to hide in the branches of a lone oak tree in an open field, reasoning that it was so prominent a spot that it would not be searched. Later Charles travelled in disguise as the servant of Miss Jane Lane, sister of a royalist colonel, and finally – some six weeks after Worcester – made it to Shoreham, west Sussex, from where he fled to safety in France aboard a coal brig, the *Surprise*.

Below: Before his failed invasion of England, Charles II was crowned at Scone in 1651.

CHAPTER FOUR

THE RESTORATION OF THE STUARTS

1660–1714

The execution of King Charles I on 30 January 1649 appeared to be the end for the royal house of Stuart. Indeed, when Parliament abolished the monarchy on 17 March 1649, it seemed to mark the point of no return for all of England's royal rulers. However, after the death of Oliver Cromwell in 1658 and the apparent failure of the Commonwealth and Protectorate, Charles I's son Charles Stuart was recalled from exile in the Low Countries. He returned to London amid public rejoicing on 29 May 1660. Diarist John Evelyn recorded, 'This day came in his Majesty Charles the 2nd to London after a sad and long exile ... with a triumph of above 20,000 horse and foot, brandishing their swords and shouting with unexpressable joy: the ways strewn with flowers, the bells ringing, the streets hung with tapestry ... the windows and balconies all set with ladys, trumpets, music, and ... people flocking the streets.' Charles II was crowned on 23 April 1661.

Stuart monarchs reigned for a further 54 years. Even when Charles II's Catholic brother, James II, was overthrown and replaced according to the will of Parliament by the Protestant William III, Stuarts remained on the throne, for William was Charles II's nephew and William's wife and joint sovereign, Mary II, was James II's daughter. The Stuart line is said to have ended with the death of Mary's sister, Queen Anne, and the accession under the Act of Settlement of King George, first ruler of the House of Hanover. However, even George had a blood connection to the Stuarts, for he was the son of Sophia, Electress of Hanover, who was King James I's granddaughter.

Left: Monarchy restored, in an imposing figure. Charles II was powerfully built, standing 6ft 2in (1.88m) tall. He had black hair, an olive complexion and dark brown eyes.

CHARLES II
1660–1685

Charles Stuart, son of the executed King Charles I, arrived in London to claim the English throne on 29 May 1660, his 30th birthday. Cheering crowds lined the streets, flowers were cast in the roadway and the bells rang out in the City of London to acclaim the restoration of the English monarchy following the harsh years of the English Commonwealth and Protectorate.

Some three and a half months earlier, on 16 March, the reconstituted Long Parliament of 1640 had voted to dissolve ahead of elections. The newly elected Convention Parliament that assembled on 25 April was strongly pro-royalist and on 1 May declared that the government should be by a restored king, House of Lords and House of Commons. MPs approved Charles's restoration on the basis of the king's Declaration of Breda, in the Low Countries, which he issued on 4 April. He promised a general pardon; liberty of conscience in religion; to pay the army and take soldiers into his own service on the same conditions they presently enjoyed; and to entrust Parliament with settling disputes over land ownership arising from the troubles of the previous 20 years. On this basis, the Lords and Commons proclaimed Charles king on 8 May.

CHARLES II, KING OF ENGLAND, SCOTLAND AND IRELAND, 1660–1685

Birth: 29 May 1630, St James's Palace, London
Father: Charles I
Mother: Henrietta Maria
Accession: 30 Jan 1649
Coronation: 1 Jan 1651, Scone (Scotland); 23 April 1661 (Westminster Abbey)
Queen: Catherine of Braganza (m. 21 May 1662; d. 1705)
Succeeded by: His brother, James II
Greatest achievement: Regaining and retaining the crown
4 April 1660: Charles Stuart issues Declaration of Breda
8 May 1660: Parliament proclaims him King Charles II
29 May 1660: Charles enters London
24 March 1663: Grants North American lands of 'Carolina' to eight wealthy noblemen
8 July 1663: Grants royal charter to Rhode Island colony
2–6 Sept 1666: Great Fire of London
1678: Former priest Titus Oates alleges Catholic plot to kill Charles
1681: Grants lands of Pennsylvania to Quaker William Penn
1683: Rye House Plot foiled
Death: 6 Feb 1685. Buried in King Henry VIII Chapel, Westminster Abbey

A FINE CORONATION

Colour, spectacle and glamour were emphasized in Charles's coronation on 23 April 1661. Wearing robes of crimson velvet and cloth of gold, riding a horse fitted with a gold- and pearl-encrusted saddle, he rode through the city in a magnificent procession past splendid theatrical tableaux, from Tower Hill to Westminster Abbey.

London diarist Samuel Pepys attended the Coronation ceremony in the Abbey. It was so crowded, he reported, that he had to take his place some seven hours before the service began. He saw, 'The king in his robes, bare headed, which was very fine … in the Quire at the high altar he passed all the ceremonies of the Coronacion … the crowne being put upon his head, a great shout begun … and three times the King-at-armes … proclaimed that if any one could show any reason why Ch.Steward should not be King of

Below: King Charles II's coronation procession. New crowns and regalia were made at a cost of £12,000.

Above: On the night of the Great Fire of London, flames illuminate Ludgate and old St Paul's. This anonymous oil painting of the disaster was made c.1670.

England, that he should come and speak'. Afterwards silver medals were thrown into the congregation, but Pepys was unable to get hold of one. A splendid coronation feast followed, then as the day ended a great thunderstorm burst over Whitehall – which Pepys interpreted as a good omen for the new king's reign.

A LOVER OF PLEASURE

While he was astute in his handling of parliamentary, military and religious factions, and a convinced believer in the sacredness of absolute monarchy, Charles was not a pious or particularly serious man. He was charismatic and charming and a passionate collector of mistresses, even after his 1662 wedding to the Portuguese Infanta, Catherine of Braganza. He once declared that he did not believe God would 'Make a man miserable only for taking a little pleasure out of the way'.

PLAGUE AND FIRE

There were many among the new king's population who looked with horror at his court's devotion to pleasure. When two disasters struck England within years of the Restoration, Puritan critics could claim that the events were evidence of God's displeasure at the hasty abandonment of England's great republican experiment.

Bubonic plague was a regular threat to London's crowded streets from the start of the 17th century onwards, but it hit with particular virulence following a heat wave in June 1665. Charles, his court and Parliament fled to Oxford, while the exchequer was moved to Surrey. In London, fires burned in the streets in an attempt to cleanse the air. As many as 70,000 people died.

Then on 2–6 September 1666 the Great Fire of London ravaged the capital. Beginning in the early hours of 2 September at the king's bakery in

Above: The plague was a recurrent threat. Charles was happy to revive the traditional practice of royal cure by laying on hands.

Pudding Lane, close to London Bridge, the fire was whipped by a strong east wind and spread quickly through London's narrow streets of tightly packed wooden houses. Pepys wrote, 'We saw the fire as only one entire arch of fire…it made me weep to see it. The churches, houses, and all on fire and flaming at once, and horrid noise the flames made, and the cracking of houses at their ruin'.

The Great Fire made 100,000 people homeless and destroyed 13,000 houses and 87 parish churches as well as St Paul's Cathedral. On 4 September King Charles did his reputation no harm by turning out to fight the fire with his people in the streets. He could be seen, clothes sodden and face blackened with smoke, working side by side with the desperate Londoners. He also sent food to the poverty-stricken and money to boost fire control efforts. Afterwards he promised the devastated people of London that he would build a splendid new city of stone and brick.

OAK APPLE DAY

After Charles's triumphant entry into London on 29 May 1660, Parliament voted that this day should be kept as a national holiday; in the words of diarist Samuel Pepys, 'As a day of thanksgiving for our redemption from tyranny and the king's return to his Government'. It was named Oak Apple Day, a reference to Charles's escape from the troops of the Parliamentary army when he hid in an oak tree near Boscobel House, Shropshire, following the Battle of Worcester, in 1651.

Above: Protective species that sheltered a king, the oak tree is celebrated as a symbol of endurance and of Englishness.

THE MERRY MONARCH
RESTORATION LIFE

 On 21 May 1662 Charles II married the pious Catholic princess Catherine of Braganza, daughter of the King of Portugal. Under the marriage treaty, which cemented an English-Portuguese-French alliance against Spain, Catherine would maintain her allegiance to the Catholic Church while agreeing that any children of the marriage should be raised as Protestants. On the wedding day, the royal couple went through two ceremonies. The first, conducted in private, was a Catholic one. The second, conducted in public, was the official Church of England rite.

MANY MISTRESSES

Queen Catherine brought a vast dowry to the marriage, which included £360,000 and the Portuguese overseas possessions of Bombay and Tangier. Charles, for his part, promised that he intended to be a good husband. However, marriage vows did not prevent the promiscuous king from continuing to pursue his favourite sport of collecting mistresses. One of these, Lady Castlemaine, was a long-standing lover whom Charles had met before the Restoration, at Breda. At his wedding she was appointed among Queen Catherine's ladies of the bedchamber, despite the fact that she had borne Charles a son the previous year. Subsequently, Charles recognized several children of this liaison as his own, and according to royal convention gave them the name 'Fitzroy'.

Another mistress of the early years was Lucy Walter, the daughter of a prominent Welsh family and 'Brown, beautiful and bold' according to diarist John Evelyn. She was intimate with the king in 1648–51, and her son of 1649, initially known as 'James Fitzroy', later became James Scott, Duke of Monmouth, who was championed as a possible Protestant successor to King Charles in his latter years.

Another mistress was Italian duchess Hortense Mancini, to whom Charles gave rooms in St James's Palace, where he visited her nightly. According to court gossips, he was drawn as much by her expertise in the arts of love as by her alluring dark beauty.

Among Charles's most celebrated lovers was actress Nell Gwynn, who became the king's mistress in 1670. She reportedly called him Charles the Third on the grounds that he was 'The third Charley' she had accepted into her bed. The following year the king also took up with a French Catholic noblewoman, Louise de Kéroualle. When

Above: Restoration gallant. The king's roguish love of pleasure is suggested in this portrait by Peter Lely (1618–80).

the outspoken Nell Gwynn had her carriage jostled by a crowd who had mistaken her for her unpopular Catholic rival, she exclaimed, 'Pray good people be civil, I am the Protestant whore'.

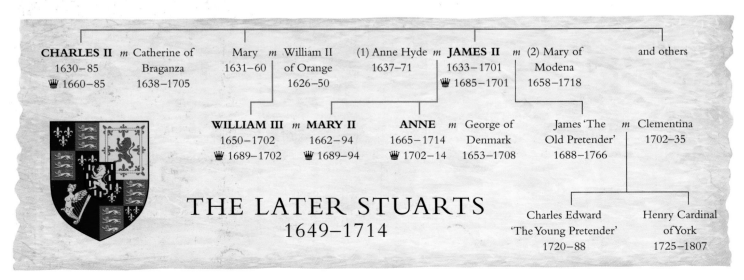

CHARLES II	m	Catherine of	Mary	m	William II	(1) Anne Hyde	m	JAMES II	m	(2) Mary of		and others
1630–85		Braganza	1631–60		of Orange	1637–71		1633–1701		Modena		
♛ 1660–85		1638–1705			1626–50			♛ 1685–1701		1658–1718		

	WILLIAM III	m	MARY II		ANNE	m	George of		James 'The	m	Clementina
	1650–1702		1662–94		1665–1714		Denmark		Old Pretender'		1702–35
	♛ 1689–1702		♛ 1689–94		♛ 1702–14		1653–1708		1688–1766		

THE LATER STUARTS
1649–1714

Charles Edward	Henry Cardinal
'The Young Pretender'	of York
1720–88	1725–1807

Above: Barbara Villiers, Lady Castlemaine. Charles II reputedly spent his first night as king in her company. Samuel Pepys reported her exceptional beauty.

Above: 'Pretty, witty Nell'. Nell Gwynn was the only one of Charles's mistresses to be popular with the public. She was widely liked for her impudence and indiscretions.

SPORT AND GAMES

Charles was also a lover of sports. Before the English Restoration, when he was crowned King by the Scots at Scone in 1651, he rounded off the celebrations that followed a vast banquet by playing a round of golf. He also pioneered yachting in England. His first taste of the sport came when he received a small racing yacht, the *Mary*, from the City of Amsterdam as a present to mark the Restoration. He himself then designed a larger version that was christened the *Jamie*. On 1 October 1661 he raced the *Jamie* against his brother, the Duke of York, sailing a Dutch yacht called the *Bezan* from Greenwich to Gravesend and back again. Charles's *Jamie* won by a distance of 3 miles (5km).

At Newmarket in Suffolk the king was a frequent visitor to the racecourse, and rode his own stallion, 'Old Rowley', in races on the heath. On 14 October 1671 the king won a race over 4 miles (6.5km) on the Newmarket course. He built a summer house, afterwards called 'the King's Chair', from which he could watch the races – and began his own racing establishment, the Palace House Stables. His love of entertainment, coupled with his easy-going manner and enjoyment of pleasure, won him the nickname the 'Merry Monarch'.

RESTORATION THEATRE

Charles II was a keen and appreciative patron of the arts and sciences. London's theatres had been closed by the Puritan establishment in the years of the Commonwealth and the Protectorate. In 1662, Charles granted patents to Thomas Killigrew and Sir William Davenant to open theatres. Thomas Killigrew inaugurated the *Theatre Royal* in Covent Garden on 7 May 1663 with a performance of *The Humorous Lieutenant* by John Fletcher and Francis Beaumont.

After the years of repression, London's theatres burst forth once more in the vibrant stage scene of 'Restoration theatre'. The works of playwrights John Dryden (appointed Poet Laureate in 1668), Beaumont and Fletcher, and William Wycherley were widely performed and praised to the skies. Henry Purcell was appointed court composer in 1677.

Below: Londoners rejoiced at the reopening of the city's theatres at the Restoration. This engraving shows the Duke's Theatre, Lincoln's Inn Fields, in Charles II's time.

A ROYAL SOCIETY OF SCIENTISTS

The reign of Charles saw a powerful surge of scientific achievement. Robert Boyle, Robert Hooke, Isaac Newton, Edmond Halley and John Flamsteed were all at work during this period. This achievement was encouraged by the king, who granted a charter to a group of scientists to found the Royal Society on 22 April 1662.

In 1675 Charles appointed Flamsteed the first 'Astronomer Royal' and in 1675–76 built the Greenwich Royal Observatory. Boyle published his *The Sceptical Chemist* in 1661; Newton demonstrated his theories on the laws of gravity at the Royal Society in 1683–4, and in 1687 he published his masterwork, the *Philosophiae Naturalis Principia Mathematica* ('Mathematical Principles of Natural Philosophy' – generally known as the *Principia*).

Hooke experimented with early reflecting microscopes and published his *Micrographia* ('Small Drawings') in 1665. He was one of the earliest pioneers of the theory of evolution.

CHARLES II AND THE 'NEW WORLD'
THE GROWTH OF NORTH AMERICA

The England of Charles II was in fierce competition with the Netherlands for control of maritime trade around the globe and in particular the sea transport of West African slaves to North America.

'NEW AMSTERDAM'

In 1664 an English privateering fleet took possession of the Dutch fur-trading post at 'New Amsterdam' on the Hudson River in North America. This settlement, at the foot of Manhattan Island, had been established for almost 40 years, since 1625. In 1664 its Dutch director-general, Peter Stuyvesant, offered no resistance to the English occupiers.

However, the following year, in the wake of this attack and English raids on Dutch slave-trading posts in West Africa, the Dutch declared war on England.

Below: James, Duke of York, ruled the territory of 'New York' with absolute authority under the 'duke's laws'.

The war lasted just two years. It began with a great English victory, as James, the Duke of York, sunk 16 Dutch vessels and captured nine more in the Battle of Lowestoft. However, in June and August 1666 ferocious sea battles caused vast losses of men and ships on both sides. England's position was further weakened by the effects of the 1665 Great Plague and the 1666 Great Fire of London. Then in 1667, with the English navy staying in port to conserve resources, the Dutch struck a humiliating blow: sailing brazenly up the Thames estuary, they burst into Chatham harbour, sunk four warships and left with no less a prize than the *Royal Charles*, the Duke of York's flagship. Both England and the Netherlands were by now keen to broker peace, and the Treaty of Breda ending the war was signed on 31 July 1667.

Under the treaty, the Dutch gave England 'New Amsterdam' and the surrounding area, while in return they gained possession of Surinam in South America. The English renamed the Manhattan Island settlement 'New York' in honour of the king's brother James, the Duke of York. The two principal

Above: A European treaty with major consequences for America. The Dutch ceded the future 'New York' to England under the Treaty of Breda, 31 July 1667.

boroughs were King's (for King Charles) and Queen's (for Queen Catherine); the first is now called Brooklyn but the second has retained its original name.

The wider surrounding area was the former Dutch colony of New Netherland, established by the Dutch West India Company in 1624 at Fort Orange (modern Albany, New York state) to provide access to the lucrative trade in furs from the Great Lakes. Charles gave this land to the Duke of York in return for an annual 'rent' of 40 beaver skins.

The Duke of York granted control of land between the Hudson and Delaware rivers to John, Lord Berkeley and Sir George Carteret. They named the land 'New Jersey' after the island of Jersey in the English Channel where Carteret was born and where he had served as Lieutenant Governor. The territory later passed into the hands of Quaker entrepreneurs, one of whom was William Penn, founder of Pennsylvania.

THE COLONY OF CAROLINA

Shortly after the Restoration, on 24 March 1663, Charles granted a wide tract of North America to a group of eight nobles, including Lord Ashley, the Duke of Albemarle, the Earl of Clarendon and the New Jersey founders Lord Berkeley and Sir George Carteret. These men founded the colony of Carolina (from the Latin form of their monarch's name). Lord Ashley's secretary, the philosopher John Locke, wrote the constitution for the new colony.

Two years later, the area of the colony, which already ran from the Atlantic to the Pacific, was further extended. In this form the vast landholding included all the following US states: North and South Carolina, Alabama, Arkansas, Arizona, Georgia, Louisiana, Mississippi, New Mexico, Oklahoma and Tennessee, as well as parts of southern California, Nevada, Florida, Missouri and of Mexico.

A RELIGIOUS HAVEN

In 1663 Charles granted a royal charter to Baptist clergyman John Clarke for the colony of Rhode Island. The colony had been founded in 1636, by Roger Williams, a religious émigré. Charles's

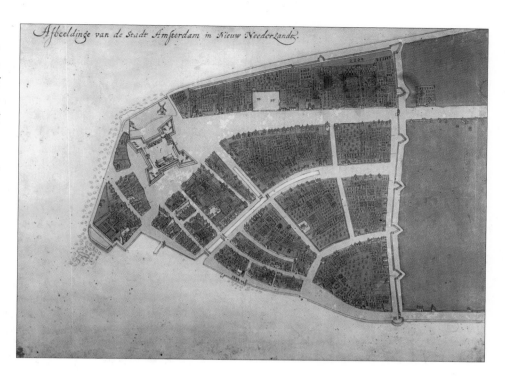

charter guaranteed the Rhode Island colonists freedom of religious conscience: 'No person within the said colony, at any time hereafter shall be any wise molested, punished, disquieted, or called in question, for any differences in opinion in matters of religion'.

In 1679 Charles declared the land of New Hampshire a separate royal province. The colony had been founded under King Charles I in the 1620s, and

Above: Manhattan as it was. This view of New Amsterdam is from 1660, before the settlement passed into English hands.

named New Hampshire in 1629. For almost 40 years prior to the 1679 declaration, New Hampshire was governed as part of Massachussetts Bay Colony. English colonization of North America was therefore well advanced by the end of Charles II's reign.

A CHRISTIAN COMMONWEALTH: PENNSYLVANIA

In 1681 King Charles made a large grant of land west of the Delaware river to his friend William Penn, a leading Quaker. The grant was by way of cancelling a large debt Charles owed to Penn's father, Admiral Sir William Penn.

On the land so given, William Penn founded the American Commonwealth of Pennsylvania (named in honour of his father). It was intended to be a refuge for Quakers and other religious groups exiled by European persecution, and an explicit attempt to create a perfect Christian commonwealth.

In the same year, Penn also received the 'lower counties' (the lands that became the modern US state of Delaware) as a

grant from the Duke of York. The city of Philadelphia was laid out on a grid pattern according to Penn's instructions.

Above: At court in London, a soberly dressed William Penn (right) receives the charter for Pennsylvania from the king.

THE REBUILDING OF LONDON
AFTER THE GREAT FIRE OF 1666

 The Great Fire of London broke out in a baker's shop in Pudding Lane on the night of 2 September 1666 and destroyed most of the City.

A NEW CITY

Just days after the fire, Charles II was presented with three separate plans for reconstruction. One was drawn up by chemist and architect Robert Hooke, one by diarist and courtier John Evelyn, who had already served on pre-fire commissions for improving London's streets (1662), and one by Christopher Wren, Savilian Professor of Astronomy at Oxford University (from 1661), who had already designed the Sheldonian Theatre in Oxford (1662).

All three plans recommended regularizing the street layout, but in the event none was adopted, principally because London's landlords were unwilling to countenance changes that would lead to drops in rent, and there

Above: Sir Christopher Wren, with St Paul's behind. Wren was a Mason, and full Masonic rites attended the laying of the St Paul's foundation stone in June 1675.

was a shortage of money to offer them compensation. In 1667 a Rebuilding Act provided for certain streets to be made wider, set improved standards for house-building and imposed a tax on coal imports to raise funds for rebuilding. This tax was increased in another act of 1670. Charles also gave a boost to redevelopment by repealing the tax on hearthstones. Hooke and Wren both played central roles in the reconstruction of the city. Hooke was appointed city surveyor for the building of houses, while Wren was made surveyor-general of the king's works in 1669.

In this capacity Wren supervised the rebuilding of St Paul's Cathedral and of London's parish churches. Although 87 churches had been destroyed, only 52 were rebuilt because smaller parishes were amalgamated. Wren personally designed or approved each one.

'RESURGAM'

Wren's new St Paul's Cathedral was built to the third design he produced: his second and favourite design was approved by King Charles but had to be dropped because of opposition to it among the canons of St Paul's. Building began in 1675 following the issue of a royal warrant that gave Wren liberty 'To make some variations rather ornamental than essential, as from time to time he should see proper'. For the foundation stone, Wren asked a workman to find a flat piece from the remains of the first cathedral. The stone, which Wren laid himself, was a fragment of a grave headstone bearing the Latin inscription

Below: Wren's masterpiece. The section, elevation and half-plan of the architect's third and final design for St Paul's.

Resurgam ('I will rise again'). St Paul's Cathedral was not finished until 1710 – although the structure was complete enough for the first service to be held there in 1697. Its magnificent dome became a London landmark.

THE SUCCESSION QUESTION

In the 1670s, after Queen Catherine had had several miscarriages, Charles's subjects began to suspect that he would not produce a legitimate heir, despite the fact that he had maintained a regular and generous output of illegitimate offspring with his many mistresses. The likelihood that the throne would pass to Charles's brother James, Duke of York, began to seem a potential calamity after James married the Catholic Mary of Modena in 1673 and word spread that the duke had himself secretly converted to Catholicism.

The staunchly Protestant Whig party in the Commons repeatedly sought to bar the Duke of York from the accession, but although bills were voted through in the Commons, Charles outmanoeuvred the Whigs to prevent them becoming law. However, the king was unable to prevent the passing of severe laws that barred Catholics from

Parliament and even from residing in London, and the Catholic Duke of York was sent into exile in 1679–80.

An assassination plan was uncovered in 1683. The Rye House Plot took its name from a house used by Charles and the Duke of York when they travelled from London to Newmarket in Suffolk to attend horse-racing meetings. The plan was to seize the royal pair and place Charles's illegitimate son, the Protestant Duke of Monmouth, on the throne. When the plot was uncovered, Monmouth, Charles's son by his mistress Lucy Walter, fled into exile.

Above: Whitehall Palace and St James's Park in the 17th century. In 1678, Titus Oates claimed that 'Popish plotters' intended to kidnap the king in the park.

Meanwhile in 1670, 1678 and 1681 Charles made secret deals allying himself with the French king Louis XIV in return for substantial payments. The first agreement contained an explosive clause in which Charles promised to announce his conversion to Catholicism and to accept military and financial aid from the French if – as it surely would – this provoked unrest among his subjects. Historians are divided over whether Charles was committed to these agreements or whether he played Louis along for the financial benefit, which was significant enough to make him independent of Parliament for the last four years of his reign, 1681–5.

'A PRETTY, WITTY KING'

Charles was remembered indulgently by his subjects as the 'Merry Monarch', celebrated in the Earl of Rochester's lines, 'We have a pretty witty king, Whose word no man relies on; Who never said a foolish thing, nor ever did a wise one.' Although he has been criticised for lacking seriousness of mind and application to the affairs of government, he did succeed in stabilizing the monarchy after the troubled years of the Commonwealth and Protectorate.

A CATHOLIC AT THE LAST

King Charles II died on 6 February 1685. On his deathbed he secretly converted to the Catholicism espoused by his wife and feared by his subjects. He was severely unwell for four days after suffering a stroke, but maintained his good humour and before he died made his peace with his queen and many illegitimate offspring. Queen Catherine, who had loved him powerfully throughout his years of philandering, sat patiently with him during the illness, but was absent at the end because she grieved so fiercely. When she sent an apology for not being present, the king exclaimed, 'Alas, poor woman. She beg my pardon? I beg hers with all my heart!'

Above: In his final hours, Charles found peace and listened to his conscience.

JAMES II AND VII
1685–1688

 The Catholic succession to King Charles II's throne that had been so feared and agitated against by the Whigs in Parliament became reality on 6 February 1685. The king's avowedly Catholic brother, James, was crowned in Westminster Abbey on 23 April and almost at once had to deal with a Protestant challenge to his authority.

PROTESTANT REBELLION

Charles's illegitimate son, the Duke of Monmouth, landed at Lyme Regis on 11 June with a mere 82 supporters to stake his claim as the Protestant heir to the throne. Although he managed to gather a force of 4,000-odd soldiers, his army was routed by royalists at the Battle of Sedgemoor on 6 July.

Meanwhile the Presbyterian Earl of Argyll returned from exile in the Low Countries to try to provoke a Scottish uprising. He did raise an army of around 1,500 – largely from his own Clan Campbell – but, faced with royalist troops, Argyll was captured and the rebellion melted away.

Above: James II's three years on the throne were a brief interlude between life as a prince, before, and a long exile, afterwards.

King James was triumphant – and secure. Argyll was beheaded in Edinburgh on 30 June. Monmouth begged for his life but was despatched in a horribly bungled execution on 15 July in which six strokes of the axe were required to kill the duke.

In the wake of these revolts James greatly expanded the army and granted command of new regiments to Catholic officers, especially in Ireland. This latter issue provoked a row with Parliament, which the king prorogued in November 1685. It did not meet again during his brief reign.

JAMES II AND VII, KING OF ENGLAND, SCOTLAND AND IRELAND, 1685–1688

Birth: 14 Oct 1633

Father: Charles I

Mother: Henrietta Maria

Accession: 6 Feb 1685

Coronation: 23 April 1685, Westminster Abbey

Wives: (1) before accession married to Anne Hyde (m. 3 Sept 1660; d. 31 March 1671); (2) Mary of Modena (m. 30 Sept 1673; d. 7 May 1718)

Succeeded by: His daughter Mary II and his son-in-law Prince William of Orange

Greatest achievement: Putting down anti-Catholic revolts in 1685

6 July 1685: Battle of Sedgemoor: defeat of Duke of Monmouth

15 July 1685: Monmouth executed

4 April 1687: James issues Declaration of Indulgence

10 June 1688: Birth of King James's son, Prince James Francis Edward

30 June 1688: Nobles call on William of Orange to invade

5 Nov 1688: William of Orange lands at Torbay

23 Dec 1688: Formally deposed as king by Parliament

Death: 6 Sept 1701, in exile at St Germain, France

PRINCE OR FOUNDLING?

Protestant opponents of the Catholic King James II drew comfort from the fact that his only feasible heirs were Protestant. None of the 10 children of James and his queen Mary of Modena survived infancy, and his two surviving daughters from his previous marriage to Anne Hyde, Mary and Anne, had both made marriages to important Protestant royals; Mary to Prince William of Orange and Anne to Prince George of Denmark.

On 10 June 1688 all that changed as Queen Mary gave birth to a healthy boy, later given a Catholic christening as James Francis Edward and a powerful godfather in Pope Innocent XI. A Catholic succession was again a possibility. Some Protestants refused to accept this unwelcome development: they argued that the infant was not Mary's own, but was a foundling child who had been smuggled into the palace in a warming pan. Mary and Anne's representatives were absent from the birth and so they could not vouch for the child.

RELIGIOUS TOLERATION

James then tried to take on the Anglican establishment. On 4 April 1687 he issued a Declaration of Indulgence that suspended all laws punishing Catholic or Protestant dissenters against the Church of England. He began to promote Catholics to positions of authority in the Privy Council, courts and universities. Some of his public statements suggested that he acted out a desire for religious toleration, others that he was truly – as his opponents feared – seeking to re-establish Catholicism as the English state religion.

Matters came to a head in 1688 when Queen Mary gave birth to a healthy son after a long succession of miscarriages and infant deaths, suddenly and unexpectedly raising the prospect of a Catholic succession to the throne.

Above: The Duke of Monmouth begs for his life before the king. Victorian artist John Pettie painted this dramatic canvas.

Earlier James had ordered his Declaration of Indulgence to be reissued and read in churches, and when the Archbishop of Canterbury and six bishops wrote a petition asking him to withdraw the order, he had them cast into the Tower of London and prosecuted for seditious libel.

On 30 June all seven churchmen were acquitted of the charge. It became clear that public opinion had swung decisively against the king, for crowds on the London streets cheered the release of the bishops and bonfires were lit to celebrate their freedom. On the very same day, seven leading Protestant noblemen wrote to Prince William of Orange – husband of Princess Mary, the king's eldest daughter by his first marriage to Anne Hyde – asking him to invade and so secure Protestantism against the Catholic threat.

Prince William landed at Torbay with 15,000 troops on 5 November. The men of the West Country rose in support. A royalist army marched as far as Salisbury but was decimated by senior desertions. James fled back to London.

On 11 December, after William had marched into the capital and begun negotiations, James took flight again. As he crossed the Thames at Vauxhall, he let the Great Seal fall into the water. He got as far as Faversham and took ship for France, but was arrested and returned to London. Finally, William ordered him to leave and he escaped to France on 23 December 1688.

Below: In 1688 the Archbishop of Canterbury and six bishops were sent to the Tower of London on charges of seditious libel.

THE 'GLORIOUS REVOLUTION'
CONSTITUTIONAL MONARCHY AND 1688

When William of Orange and Princess Mary, daughter of King James II, jointly acceded to the throne on 13 February 1689, it marked the first time in English history that a royal succession had been settled not by hereditary right, military might or possession of the crown and treasury, but by the will of the two Houses of Parliament.

CONSORT OR KING?

On 23 December 1688 – the day that King James II succeeded in escaping to France – the peers and bishops of the House of Lords asked William to assume the duties of government. William summoned all the surviving MPs from the reign of Charles II to sit in the Commons. William turned down a suggestion that he should claim the throne himself by right of conquest.

On 28 January 1689 the Commons declared that James II's flight to France was an abdication of the government and that the throne was therefore vacant. The Protestant Whigs in the

Below: An allegory of the 'Glorious Revolution'. The pope (right) is offended, but Magna Carta and Liberty approve.

House of Commons were largely in favour of the throne passing to William and Mary, but in the Lords the Tory supporters of absolute monarchy were concerned to safeguard the principle of hereditary succession. Tory suggestions that Mary should rule alone (having inherited the throne as King James II's daughter), or that William and Mary should govern as regents until James II died, came to nothing. On 3 February 1689 William declared that he would not agree to rule as regent or as Mary's consort. He demanded the full power and sovereignty of a monarch, jointly held with his wife.

THE BILL OF RIGHTS

On 12 February 1689 Princess Mary arrived in London after travelling from the Netherlands, and both houses of Parliament agreed a 'Declaration of Rights'. When on the following day William and Mary accepted the terms of this declaration and were elevated to the throne as joint rulers, a new kind of royal government was brought into being: constitutional monarchy.

The Declaration of Rights, which was made formal in a Bill of Rights passed on 16 December 1689, made a

Above: A detail from James Thornhill's Painted Hall at Greenwich shows William and Mary enthroned in regal splendour.

number of ground-breaking changes to the relationship between monarch and Parliament. The monarch was barred from keeping a standing army, and Parliament had final authority in declaring war, raising taxes and passing laws. Free elections to Parliament would be held every three years, and MPs would be guaranteed freedom of speech. Subjects also had the right to petition the monarch on matters of concern. All Protestants had the right to carry arms for self-defence, to enjoy freedom from cruel and unusual punishments and excessive bail, and to live free from fines imposed without trial.

The new settlement also safeguarded the Protestant faith and made explicit a connection between Protestantism and the liberty of Englishmen. The Bill of Rights declared that, 'It hath pleased

THE CIVIL LIST

Under the Civil List Act 1697 Parliament granted William III annual funds of £700,000 for the rest of his life. These were to cover the king's royal and civil expenses.

The Civil List grant replaced an earlier parliamentary voting of funds, made on William's accession with Mary in 1689, of £600,000 annually. The custom of the Civil List was new: previous monarchs were expected to find money for these expenses from hereditary revenues and taxes. However, many earlier kings and queens had had far greater freedom to raise tax income without needing parliamentary approval.

Almighty God to make [William] the glorious instrument of delivering this kingdom from popery and arbitrary power'. Under the bill, all Catholics – including James II and his offspring – and all those married to Catholics were barred from the succession. The document declared, 'It hath been found be experience that it is inconsistent with the safety and welfare of this Protestant Kingdom to be governed by a popish prince'. When William and Mary were

Below: Queen and king. A beadwork bag made by Mary for William celebrates their loving relationship and their joint rule.

Above: A new relationship between monarch and subjects. The Bill of Rights is presented to William and Mary.

crowned on 11 April in Westminster Abbey, they swore new oaths that required them to uphold 'The Protestant reformed religion established by law' and to govern in accordance with the 'Statutes of Parliament'.

The Bill also specified the future Protestant succession: first, through the heirs of Queen Mary II, then through Mary's sister Princess Anne and her heirs and then through any heirs of William III by a later marriage.

SCOTTISH RIGHTS

In Scotland a Convention of Scottish Estates drew up a similar document to the declaration, called a Claim of Right, and passed it on 11 April 1689.

The document declared that James had 'Forfeited the right to the crown' since as a 'Professed papist' he had 'Assumed regal power without ever taking the oath required by law'; that is, 'To swear to maintain the Protestant religion'. He had also, the Claim declared, 'Invaded the fundamental constitution of the Kingdom, and altered it from a legal limited monarchy to an arbitrary despotic power'. Therefore, the Estates said, the throne was vacant.

The Claim, like its English counterpart, barred Catholics from the throne; it also declared the printing of 'popish books' to be illegal and outlawed the practice of sending children abroad for a Catholic education.

William and Mary accepted the Scottish crown on 11 May 1689 in Whitehall. However, they faced considerable opposition to their rule there, particularly in the Highlands, where allegiance to Catholicism and the House of Stuart was strong.

WILLIAM III AND MARY II
1689–1694

 On 13 February 1689 William and Mary were jointly offered the throne under a Bill of Rights agreed in both Lords and Commons that made the monarchy subject to Parliament. On 11 April 1689 they were crowned England's joint rulers King William III and Queen Mary II. Almost at once they faced opposition in Scotland from those loyal to King James II. These opponents were called 'Jacobites' from the Latin form, *Jacobus*, of 'James'.

BONNIE DUNDEE
James II was in exile at the Versailles court of the French king, Louis XIV. He gave his backing to Scots nobleman John Graham, Viscount Dundee, to be his military commander in Scotland. Just two days after William and Mary's coronation, Dundee raised the Jacobite standard in Scotland. Rebels loyal to the ousted king began to muster under the command of this charismatic figure known as 'Bonnie Dundee', a veteran of 1679 struggles

Above: Protestants ride to triumph. American artist Benjamin West painted this view of William's victory at the Boyne.

against Presbyterians in the cause of Charles II. On 27 July 1689 Dundee led a force of highlanders in a famous victory over a royalist army commanded by General Hugh Mackay at Killiecrankie. This could have proved a turning point, but after the battle Dundee died from a musket shot he received in conflict, and without his leadership the Jacobite cause foundered. The royalist forces regrouped and on 21 August at Dunkeld inflicted a major defeat on the Jacobites that was decisive in the short term.

William demanded oaths of loyalty from the leaders of the Highland clans. When the MacDonald clan chief Alastair MacIain failed to make the oath by the required deadline, troops of the Argyll regiment inflicted a terrible massacre on the MacDonalds at Glencoe on 13 February 1692. Public outrage at this incident combined with the fact that William did not try to punish those responsible for the massacre, undermined his popularity.

IRISH WAR
In Ireland the struggle to secure the Protestant succession provoked a two-year war. James II landed at Kinsale, County Cork, on 12 March 1689 to reclaim his throne. His 20,000-strong

---

WILLIAM III, KING OF ENGLAND, SCOTLAND AND IRELAND AND PRINCE OF ORANGE, 1689–1702

Birth: 4 Nov 1650, Binnenhof Palace, The Hague

Father: William II, Prince of Orange

Mother: Princess Mary, daughter of Charles I

Accession: 13 Feb 1689

Coronation: 11 April 1689, Westminster Abbey

Queen: Mary (m. 4 Nov 1677; d. 28 Dec 1694)

Succeeded by: His sister-in-law Anne

Greatest achievement: Battle of the Boyne

27 July 1689: Jacobites clash with royalists at Killiecrankie

21 Aug 1689: Royalists victorious at the Battle of Dunkeld

1689–90: Bloody siege of Londonderry

1 July 1690: Defeats James II at the Battle of the Boyne

3 Oct 1691: Irish 'Williamite War' ends with Treaty of Limerick

13 Feb 1692: Glencoe Massacre of MacDonald clansmen

31 Dec 1694: A griefstricken King William breaks down before Parliament

Feb 1695: William acknowledges Princess Anne as his heir

30 July 1700: Anne's only son, William Duke of Gloucester, dies aged 11

6 Sept 1701: Death of exiled King James II at St Germain

Death: 8 March 1702. Buried in Westminster Abbey

French army was boosted by vast
numbers of Irish Catholics loyal to his
rule. On 4 May 1689 the Irish parliament in Dublin declared the country to
be behind James. At first James swept
Protestant opposition aside, but at
Londonderry (Derry), Ulster, he found
the gates closed against him. In December
he embarked on a siege of around 105
days. Thousands of lives were lost and
the enduring Irish Protestant slogan of
'No Surrender' was born as the city
endured the siege until it was lifted by
a relief ship.

William landed at Carrickfergus on
24 June 1690. On 1 July, at the head of
a vast army of 36,000 soldiers that
included Dutch, Germans, French
Huguenots and Ulster Protestants as
well as Englishmen, he inflicted a decisive
defeat on James's army at the Battle of
the Boyne, near Drogheda. James fled to
France; William returned to England,

*Right: Major battles of the 'Williamite
war'. After victory at the Boyne, William's
army swept across southern Ireland.*

summoning John Churchill, the Duke
of Marlborough, to command royalist
forces in Ireland. The war continued for
a further 15 months until the Peace of
Limerick was signed on 3 October 1691.

A UNITED COUPLE

Although he was celebrated as the
upholder of England's Protestant destiny,
William was never really popular with
his people. He was doubtless distrusted
as a foreigner and, in sharp contrast to
the flamboyant Charles II, he had an
unattractive appearance and manner –
short and stooped with severe asthma
and a withdrawn character. Queen
Mary, by contrast, had an elegant figure
and charming manners and at 5ft 11in
(1.8m) was a full 5in (12cm) taller than
her husband. She was widely acclaimed
and proved a dutiful wife. In the normal
run of affairs, she left affairs of state and

*Above: After defeat at the Battle of the
Boyne, the former James II escapes from
Ireland by boat, bound for France.*

government to William, but when he
was abroad at war she demonstrated
fine judgement. Mary died aged just 32
from smallpox in 1694. Her devastated
husband was left to rule alone.

LONDONDERRY
1689

CARRICKFERGUS

BELFAST
ARMAGH

ENNISKILLEN
1689

Newtownbutler
1690

DUNDALK

Boyne 1690

North
Atlantic
Ocean

Aughrim
1691

ATHLONE

DUBLIN

Irish
Sea

LIMERICK
1690

WATERFORD

CORK 1690
KINSALE

⊗ William III victories
🏴 Besieged by William
🏴 Besieged by James

WILLIAM III RULES ALONE
1694–1702

William was so devastated by the death of Queen Mary in 1694 that he was overcome by his emotions in Parliament and could not make a reply when offered the condolences of MPs.

He apparently saw the queen's untimely death as God's judgment on him for his sins. He withdrew from his long-standing affair with Elizabeth Villiers, the eldest daughter of Richmond gentleman Sir Edward Villiers. It seems that it was as a parting gift that he made over to Elizabeth Villiers all King James II's landholdings in Ireland in January 1695.

To escape his grief, William threw himself into the Continental war that had been running since the creation of a Protestant 'Grand Coalition' in 1689, and in September 1695 he led the army to victory over the French at Namur. In the absence of the heirs he had hoped to produce with Queen Mary, he also formally recognized his sister-in-law, the increasingly overweight 30-year-old Princess Anne, as his successor.

JACOBITE PLOTS

In 1696 a failed Jacobite assassination plot had the effect of rallying public opinion in William's favour. The

Above: Sir Godfrey Kneller's portrait masks William's physical failings. In reality the king had a short, stooping figure.

plan, developed at the French court, was for Sir George Barclay – a former associate of 'Bonnie Dundee' – to kidnap and kill the king at Turnham Green as he returned to London from Richmond. However, the details were leaked to the royal party and the attempt was never made; Barclay escaped back to France. Afterwards Parliament passed the Act of Association, laying a requirement on all holders of public office to swear that William was 'rightful and lawful king'; and, because Jacobites made trips to the court of the French king, Louis XIV, to hatch their plans, it was declared high treason to travel from France to England without official authority.

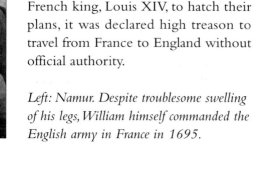

Left: Namur. Despite troublesome swelling of his legs, William himself commanded the English army in France in 1695.

The Continental war came to an end in 1697 with the Treaty of Ryswick (on the outskirts of the Hague), signed on 20 September between William III, Louis XIV of France and Spain's Charles II. For the first time Louis — who had previously viewed James II as the rightful English king — accepted William as king of England. Other terms of the treaty saw Louis restore most of the conquests he had made since the start of the war in 1689 and recognize the independence of Savoy.

Following the death of James II on 6 September 1701 at St Germain, Louis recognized James's 13-year-old son, James Francis Edward, as the rightful king of England — in direct contravention of the treaty. In England opinion swelled in favour of war with the French. The Commons had voted in April to back the Dutch against the French and in June to ally with Austria and the United Provinces — and on 7 September in the Hague William agreed to ally Britain with the Netherlands and the Holy Roman Empire.

A NEW SUCCESSION CRISIS

At home, the death of the 11-year-old Duke William of Gloucester, only son of William's recognized successor, Princess Anne, put the Protestant succession in jeopardy. On 12 June 1701 Parliament passed the Act of Settlement, which nominated a new and unexpected Protestant heir to follow Anne. The heir was to be Sophia, Electress of Hanover, the daughter of Charles I's sister Elizabeth and her husband Frederick V the Elector Palatinate. The act made it abundantly clear where final authority now resided: in Parliament, which had the gift of the crown among its powers.

Parliament's decision was that it was better to pass the crown to a foreign royal family than to risk it falling into Catholic hands. The Act of Settlement excluded from succession any Catholics who married princesses of the Stuart line. It also tried to limit potential problems arising from giving royal power to

the Hanoverian royal line by stating that future monarchs would not be permitted to launch a war 'for the defence of dominions or territories which do not belong to the Crown of England, without the consent of Parliament'. It also stated that future monarchs would not be permitted to depart Britain without parliamentary consent. Additionally, monarchs would be prevented from appointing foreign courtiers to high position under a clause that declared that those born outside Britain might not serve on the privy council.

King William did not live to see the war with France towards which he was manoeuvring the country. On 21 February 1702 he fell from his horse and broke his collarbone after the animal stumbled over a molehill in Richmond Park. The fall plunged him into a terminal decline; he developed

Right: A king in waiting? This French portrait depicts James II's son, James Edward Stuart, in his early teens.

Above: William dies amidst courtiers in the royal bedroom. The crying figure (right) is probably the future Queen Anne.

pulmonary fever and died on 8 March In France gleeful Jacobites toasted the mole assassin, 'the little gentleman in his black velvet jacket'.

ANNE

1702–1714

Princess Anne, aged 37, plain of face and prematurely troubled by rheumatism and gout, did not make an inspiring queen when she was crowned in Westminster Abbey on 23 April 1702. She could not offer an heir: the veteran of six miscarriages and eleven stillbirths or infant mortalities, she was childless following the death of her only healthy child, Duke William of Gloucester, in 1700. Moreover, she was inexperienced in government and in affairs of state.

Nevertheless, she presided over a great period for her country, in which English armies won stunning victories over the French and re-established England as a significant European force with growing imperial possessions. The kingdoms of England and Scotland were formally joined in the Kingdom of Great Britain, and in decorative arts Britain reached a new height of elegance with the development of the Queen Anne style.

THE ACT OF UNION

The 1701 Act of Settlement that named the Protestant Hanoverian royal family as Anne's successors had provoked anger in Scotland. The Act of Security of the Kingdom, passed by the Scottish

Right: Queen Anne. The suddenness of her death seems to have caught pro-Jacobite Tories unprepared and so helped to secure the Protestant succession to the crown.

Parliament, in Edinburgh, in August 1703, declared the Scots' willingness to bar the Hanoverian accession and raised the possibility that a Stuart king could be installed in Scotland and join forces with France against England as in the days of the 'Auld Alliance'.

To rectify this situation, negotiations for the legal union of England and Scotland formally began in 1706 and on 22 July of that year a draft treaty was agreed by the 62 appointed commissioners, providing for a united kingdom with a single Parliament in Westminster, a single currency, a common union flag and, crucially, a guaranteed Protestant succession to the Hanoverian royal line. In addition, the treaty provided for the Scottish church, education and legal systems to be independent of those in England. With a few minor amendments, and thanks to the sweetening effect of a £400,000 one-off English payment to Scotland and numerous behind-the-scenes bribes – and despite Scottish public opposition strong enough to fuel riots in Edinburgh and

Glasgow – the Act of Union was passed by the Scottish Parliament on 16 January 1707. The Act received royal assent in Westminster on 6 March 1707. At a special service of thanksgiving in Sir Christopher Wren's recently completed St Paul's Cathedral on 1 May 1707,

Below: Queen of Great Britain. The articles of Anglo-Scottish union are presented to Anne in 1706.

ANNE, QUEEN OF GREAT BRITAIN AND IRELAND, 1702–1714

Birth: 6 February 1665, St James's Palace

Father: James, Duke of York (afterwards James II)

Mother: Anne Hyde

Accession: 8 March 1702

Coronation: 23 April 1702, Westminster Abbey

Husband: Prince George of Denmark (m. 28 July 1683; d. 28 Oct 1708)

Succeeded by: Her second cousin George I

Greatest achievement: Her government's creation of the Kingdom of Great Britain

1702: England at war with France

August 1704: The Battle of Blenheim

16 January 1707: Scottish Parliament approves Act of Union

6 March 1707: Royal assent to Act of Union

Death: 1 August 1714, Kensington Palace. Buried at Westminster Abbey on 24 August

Right: John Churchill, Duke of Marlborough, signs the despatch at the Battle of Blenheim in August 1704.

Queen Anne wore the insignia of the combined Order of the Garter and Order of the Thistle.

WAR WITH FRANCE

Queen Anne proved a more able and astute ruler than anyone had imagined. Her three principal ministers were all exceptionally able: John Churchill, Duke of Marlborough, who was commander-in-chief and in charge of diplomatic and military affairs; Sidney, Baron Godolphin, Lord Treasurer; and Sir Robert Harley, Secretary of State. The Continental war that was suspended following the 1697 Treaty of Ryswick reignited in 1702, largely in response to Louis XIV's backing of James' II's exiled son, James Francis Edward Stuart, in his claim for the English throne. In this conflict the English army and navy won a series of battles, most famously over Louis's army at the Battle of Blenheim (a village in south-central Germany) in August 1704, which was hailed by contemporaries as a new Agincourt or Crécy. For this great victory Churchill was rewarded with a victory parade in London on 3 January 1705 and the gift of the formerly royal manor of Woodstock, Oxfordshire, later that year. The war continued until 1713 – and one of its enduring consequences was British possession of Gibraltar in southern Spain.

QUEEN ANNE'S FAVOURITES

Before her accession Anne was very close to Sarah, wife of John Churchill, who was made Duke of Marlborough in 1702 and went on to military glory. However, after 1703, Anne's relationship with Sarah became increasingly troubled. The queen appeared to have a new favourite, Abigail Hill. Ironically she was Sarah's relation and had first gained employment as lady of the queen's bedchamber thanks to Sarah's influence. The dispute became very bitter: in 1708 Sarah even accused Anne of being a lesbian, declaring that she had 'no liking for anyone but only her own sex' and quoting a ribald poem that suggested that Abigail and Anne were involved in 'dark Deeds at night'. Anne's friendship with Sarah was cut off finally in 1710. Abigail Masham, as she became on her marriage in 1707, remained close to the queen and was created Lady Masham in 1711.

Right: This portrait of Sarah was made by Robert White (d. 1703) during the period in which she dominated Anne.

THE AILING MONARCH

Even at her accession, Queen Anne was visibly unwell, so troubled by rheumatism, weight and gout that she could walk for only a short way with the support of a stick. From at least 1707, she was virtually incapacitated by her poor health, although she continued to play her role in affairs of state. The loss of her devoted husband, Prince George of Denmark, who died in 1708, was a great blow to her. He was a dull but sensible man and she had relied greatly on his advice and support. She had a serious fever in 1713 and the following summer died on 1 August 1714, after falling into a coma. The Stuart line was ended. After some debate in cabinet, the government – in line with the Succession Act – invited Elector George of Hanover to take the throne.